THE 1970s

THE 1970s BASEBALL QUIZ BOOK

CHARLES E. SMITH

COLLIER BOOKS
A Division of Macmillan Publishing Co., Inc.
New York
COLLIER MACMILLAN PUBLISHERS
London

Macmillan Publishing Co., Inc.
866 Third Avenue, New York, N.Y. 10022
Collier Macmillan Canada, Ltd.

Library of Congress Cataloging in Publication Data

Smith, Charles E.
The 1970s baseball quiz book.
1. Baseball—United States—Miscellanea.
2. Baseball players—United States—Biography.
3. Baseball—United States—History. I. Title.
GV863.A1S64 796.357'092'2 [B] 82-1158
ISBN 0-02-029360-7 AACR2

First Collier Books Edition 1982
10 9 8 7 6 5 4 3 2 1

Printed in the United States of America

TO MY CHILDREN
CHRIS, DENISE, AND BRIAN,
WITH ALL MY LOVE

CONTENTS

ACKNOWLEDGMENTS

I believe every generation needs, if not its own heroes, then at least the conviction that it is as good or better than those that came before. The endless reminiscing of days gone by is certainly an integral part of being a baseball fan, but I had tired of hearing too many stories which revolved around the theme of "They don't make them like that any more."

Baseball in the 1970s was better than it ever had been. The players were smarter, faster, and tougher, and the records they produced prove it—records produced in spite of a grueling schedule of night games played from Toronto to Texas and from one coast to the other. Of the fourteen players who achieved 3,000 hits in this century, half of them accomplished this feat in the 1970s. That decade saw Henry Aaron break the career home-run total of the great Babe Ruth; it saw Pete Rose shatter Ty Cobb's record of nine seasons with over 200 hits and tie Wee Willie Keeler's 81-year-old NL record of hitting safely in 44 consecutive games as well; Lou Brock not only stole more bases in one season than any player before him, but he also broke the supposedly unbreakable career record of Ty Cobb. The records set in the 1970s are irrefutable and as Casey Stengel said, "You could look it up."

One of the first places to look up any baseball record would be Joe Reichler's *The Baseball Encyclopedia: The Complete and Official Record of Major League Baseball*. Another invaluable reference work is *The Great All-time Baseball Record Book: A Unique Sourcebook of Facts, Feats, and Figures*, by the same author. It is hard to imagine that any fan could exist without these two books by baseball's Boswell.

Hundreds of issues of *The Sporting News* and their annual publications, *Baseball Register, Baseball Record Book, Baseball Dope*

Book, and *Official World Series Records Book,* proved to be indispensable. Other sources that were continually consulted include the annual editions of *Street and Smith's Official Baseball Yearbook,* ten years of issues of *Baseball Digest,* issues of the *Official American League Red Book* and the *Official National League Green Book,* hundreds of issues of *Sports Illustrated,* and various other baseball magazines, relevant issues of *The New York Times,* and last but not least the yearbooks and media guides of the baseball clubs themselves. I am also indebted to the many great sports columnists who cover baseball. Finally, I read many of the relevant biographies and autobiographies.

More often than not, the material in this book comes from many of these sources at the same time—an idea from one, a fact from another checked and compared to still a few others, and so on. Where contradictions existed, and they often did, I tried to resolve them in a way that made the most sense to me. In a work consisting of so many facts and so much data, I realize that some error may have crept in somewhere, but a scrupulous reading by my colleague, Dave Biesel, saved me from several mistakes. Any that remain are my own fault.

I am grateful to Jeremiah Kaplan, president of Macmillan Publishing Co., Inc. for his encouragement; to George Walsh, editor-in-chief of the General Books Division of Macmillan, for his patience; and to Ilka Shore Cooper for seeing the manuscript through production, professionally and expeditiously. Joan Greenfield's tasteful design of a complex typographical work is appreciated.

Without the help of my wife, Denise Delaney Smith, I would not have been able to finish; I thank her for many hours of hard work.

Words will never express the debt I owe my parents, the late Charles J. and Gertrude Smith, for so much. The least of what my father did for me was to forsake his hurling and soccer and pretend to be a Brooklyn Dodger fan so that his son would come to know and understand the sport of his adopted country.

I have dedicated this book to my children—Chris, Denise, and Brian—and I hope that this is some small payment for the many hours this book took me away from them. They and their beautiful new generation were the real stars of the 1970s, and I pray that they will shine even brighter well into the next century.

THE 1970s BASEBALL QUIZ BOOK

STARS OF THE SEVENTIES

When I was a teenager growing up in New York, I went to high school for a while in the Crown Heights section of Brooklyn, not far from Ebbetts Field. I later transferred to another high school in the Chelsea neighborhood of Manhattan. Among the many similarities between the two schools was the presence of a very active betting system on baseball. It was a harmless little activity, played in increments of nickels and dimes. You chose three players and got paid something like three to one if they got four hits among them, four to one if they got five hits, and so on.

In the face of all mathematical probability, which the good Jesuits did not teach us in those days, and defying all logic, which they most emphatically did teach us, we made our choices and put down our hard-earned money, more often than not using our hearts and not our minds. The Giants fan would choose a trio such as Whitey Lockman, Alvin Dark, and Don Mueller; the Dodgers fan would opt for Jackie Robinson, Pee Wee Reese, and Roy Campanella. In my own long-lost innocence, I always put my money on Mickey Mantle and studied the season's statistics before choosing among Hank Bauer, Gene Woodling, Yogi Berra, Phil Rizzuto, Joe Collins, Billy Martin, Gil McDougald, Irv Noren, Big John Mize, and the rest of Casey's World Champions.

The guys in the class who went on to become lawyers usually made very sensible bets on more likely trios such as Ferris Fain, Mickey Mantle, and Walt Dropo, or George Kell, Stan Musial, and Ted Kluszewski. Doesn't *that* tell you something?

Choosing a list, however long or short, is at best a subjective exercise, revealing and reflecting the biases, the memories, the likes and dislikes of the one doing the choosing. To pick 70 players out of the more than 1,000 who passed through the major leagues in the 1970s is far from a scientific undertaking, and the result is one that will, I hope, cause some pleasant discussions.

Getting back to probability again, it is extremely unlikely that any fan anywhere would have chosen exactly the same 70 players. Some fans would have given more attention to pitchers, for example, than I have. Twenty-two of my 70 players are pitchers, and I do not believe that I have slighted them. Older fans may wish that more players from the early 1970s were included, and younger fans may wish that some of those stars who were just beginning their careers at the end of the decade were included. To all of them, I can only say that I have tried to achieve a chronological balance and equal representation.

Maury Allen, a national columnist for whom I have the greatest respect, recently wrote a book consisting of his personal ranking of the 100 best players since 1900. Not only did he choose the 100 best players out of over 10,000, but he even ranked them in numerical order. My comment on that thankless task may be inferred from the fact that my 70 stars of the seventies are in alphabetical sequence.

Mr. Allen has chosen Dave Winfield as the eighty-eighth best ballplayer of the twentieth century but I could not find my way clear to include him as one of my 70 stars of the seventies. Winfield has the rare combination of size, speed, power, and throwing arm that is matched only by Dave Parker. That combination, barring serious injury, should make him one of the greatest stars of the 1980s.

Winfield did hit over .300 in both 1978 and 1979, but he was still a .285 lifetime hitter at the end of the decade. He has scored over 100 runs and he has had over 100 RBIs also, but only once, and not in the same season. I agree with Mr. Allen that Dave Winfield is a good bet to become a Triple Crown winner but, for this graceful and gracious athlete, the best is yet to come. In my mind, he did not put his mark on the 1970s as indelibly as he later did on George Steinbrenner's checking account.

I have agonized over these choices so much that I am the most aware of where the flaws—at least where the grounds for the most serious disagreement—lie. Let's look at some of them, and allow me to tell you some of the reasoning that went into my selection process.

Why Boog Powell? He is a name and face known to most of the younger fans only because of his beer commercials. You will not find him on Mr. Allen's list and he may never be in the Hall of Fame, but he is on my list.

For 16 years, 14 of them with the Baltimore Orioles, the bat of John Wesley Powell was a weapon that was taken with great seriousness in the American League. During that period, he hammered his way onto the list of the top 30 home-run hitters of all time. He hit 25 or more home runs in six different years, and he went over the 100 RBI mark three times. In 1970, one of his best all-around seasons, he was named Most Valuable Player of the American League. That year, he just missed hitting .300; his 35 home runs were the fifth best in the league; his 114 RBIs were third; his 289 total bases placed him fifth, and his .549 slugging average made him second only to Carl Yastrzemski. He also fielded first base with a .992 fielding average. To wrap up the year, he hit two more home runs in the World Series to lead the Orioles to a World Championship.

No Oriole player ever hit more home runs, and only Brooks Robinson played more seasons or had more hits, runs, or RBIs as a Baltimore player.

Traded to Cleveland in 1975 at the age of 34, he reached back and hit .297 while clouting 27 more home runs and tying the club lead of 86 RBIs for the year.

For this accomplishment, he was almost selected for the AL Comeback Player of the Year Award, coming in second to his former teammate Jim Palmer. The Cleveland Baseball Writers named him their "Good Guy of the Year."

Those are some of the reasons I chose Boog Powell.

Why Roy White, now busting fences in Japan with Sadaharu Oh? Only four players appeared in more games as a Yankee than White, and they are all in the Hall of Fame. In the 1970s, he led his team in hits, doubles, and RBIs once, in runs and triples three times, and in stolen bases four times. In addition to these facts, as impressive as they are, I chose Roy White because of the way in which this gentleman went about his business, day after day, throughout the 1970s. Often criticized, always underrated, he provided a model of style and grace for players of all decades.

Why Tug McGraw? Read *Screwball,* his life story written with Joe Durso, and tell me how his irrepressible personality could be left out of any story about the 1970s. If you believe in anything, ya gotta believe in Tug.

Why Roberto Clemente, who played only three seasons during the 1970s? He hit .352, .341, and .312 in those three seasons; he was the MVP of the 1971 World Series as he led the Pirates from behind to a championship with an incredible .414 batting average; his last hit made him a member of the very exclusive 3,000-hit club.

Even with his recurrent back problem, his parathyroid condition, and a lingering malaria, there is no reason to believe that he would not have had at least three more seasons during which he would have performed at a level at least as productive as his last three seasons. If that assumption is correct, namely that he would have added 441 more hits to his 3,000, he would have been sixth on the all-time list, and very close to fifth place, held by Tris Speaker, with 3,515 career hits.

At the age of 38, he still had much to offer the world—as an athlete and as a man. At the end of an 18-year career in the major leagues, his incredible talents had finally been recognized and he had received the acclaim he so desired and so deserved. The deaths of Roberto Clemente, Lyman Bostock, and Thurman Munson make us think of all those who will not swell the rout—

> Of lads who wore their honours out,
> Runners whom renown outran
> And the name died before the man.

Dick Allen and Bobby Bonds are included, not only because of the many impressive statistics they have left on the record books but also for the impact their personalities and their characters made upon the hundreds of thousands of fans who watched them play. Possibly, there are lessons to be learned.

Seldom has baseball seen such raw talent, such precocious and multifaceted skills as these two men possessed. Allen was NL Rookie of the Year just one year after Pete Rose won the same award, and Bonds joined the San Francisco Giants just four years later.

Rose is a millionaire with a spot in Cooperstown just waiting for his retirement. He is as happy playing baseball at the age of 40 as any man or boy who ever played the game. The careers of Dick Allen and Bobby Bonds may be best summarized as a long, sad, perhaps even tragic journey: from one position to another, from one team to another, from one league to another, with not enough honors, or joy, or personal satisfaction along the way.

However, baseball is, as we are often told, "only a game," so let us not make too much of it. Whether it is an adult's game played by children or a child's game played by adults, I am not sure, so let us not make too much of that either.

For better or for worse, I have chosen my stars of the seventies, and I look forward to hearing your thoughts about them. On whom do you agree? On whom do you disagree? As Maury Allen said in his personal ranking, "Let's hear your picks. Let's not fight about it. . . . Let's just have fun."

The Stars of the Seventies quizzes are all true/false, with a bonus question thrown in. Answers are on pp. 43–73; check all true answers first, then false.

HENRY LOUIS (HANK/THE HAMMER) AARON
Born: February 5, 1934, Mobile, Alabama
Ht. 6'0"; wt. 185 lbs.
Bats and throws right

a. He is the only man in history to win three MVPs in three different decades.
b. He was hampered by minor but almost perennial injuries throughout his career.
c. He is the only NL player to hit at least 30 home runs and steal at least 30 bases in the same season.
d. Aaron did not play in the first three games of the 1974 season so that he could tie Ruth's record at his home ball park in Atlanta.
e. Cincinnati pitcher Jack Billingham threw the pitch that ended up as Aaron's 715th home run.
f. He holds the NL record for most lifetime hits, but his career major league total is over 400 hits shy of the AL record holder.

g. No player still active at the end of the 1970s was within 250 home runs of Aaron's record.
h. He hit into more double plays than any other player in history.

Question: Who was the superstar who was hurt in spring training, enabling Aaron, a rookie, to break into the Milwaukee Braves' lineup one year early?

RICHARD ANTHONY (DICK/RICH/RICHIE) ALLEN

Born: March 8, 1942, Wampum, Pennsylvania
Ht. 5'11"; wt. 187 lbs.
Bats and throws right

a. Some explain Allen's often idiosyncratic behavior as being due to the fact that he was an only child.
b. He had the best, and happiest, season of his career in 1972, when he was chosen AL MVP under manager Paul Richards.
c. In his first year in the major leagues, he was edged out of being named NL Rookie of the Year by a young Cincinnati second baseman named Pete Rose.
d. He was the first Black to play on an integrated Little Rock team.
e. Allen holds a number of all-time season records for the Phillies, including: most runs, most home runs by a rookie (right-handed batter), and total bases, extra-base hits, and slugging percentages (right-handed batter).
f. Allen holds a number of all-time season records for the Chicago White Sox, including: most home runs and highest slugging percentage (right-handed batter).
g. Allen was once traded to the Atlanta Braves, and he ended his career with the Oakland A's.
h. Often moody and very susceptible to injury, he never played in more than 140 games in one season in the 1970s.

Question: Although it happened in 1969, Allen was involved in a trade so important that it will never be forgotten. Exactly what made this trade so memorable?

DON EDWARD BAYLOR

Born: June 28, 1949, Austin, Texas
Ht. 6'1"; wt. 190 lbs.
Bats and throws right

a. He broke most of the hitting records at the university that bears his name.
b. Jim Palmer and he were the number one and two draft selections of the Baltimore Orioles in 1967.
c. He was named AL MVP in 1979.
d. He was *The Sporting News* Minor League Player of the Year in 1970.
e. He led the Baltimore Orioles in stolen bases for four years.
f. In 1976, he was traded from Baltimore to Oakland for Joe Rudi.
g. He has hit 25 or more home runs each year since 1975.
h. He has a higher combined total of home runs and stolen bases than Pete Rose.

Question: He received 347 points in the 1979 AL MVP voting. Who were the only two players who received more than 200 points?

JOHNNY LEE BENCH

Born: December 7, 1947, Oklahoma City, Oklahoma
Ht. 6′1″; wt. 215 lbs.
Bats and throws right

a. He was a pitcher and an all-state basketball player in high school.
b. He was the first draft pick of the Reds in 1965, the first year of the draft.
c. He was NL Rookie of the Year while he was still 20, and NL MVP only two years later.
d. He has hit more home runs in his career than any other player in Cincinnati history.
e. He has hit more home runs than any catcher in history.
f. He is second only to Reggie Jackson for the most RBIs in both leagues in the 1970s.
g. In the 1970s, he was the only player to lead the NL in home runs, RBIs, total bases, and slugging percentage, all in the same year.
h. In 1979, he broke the record of catching 100 or more games in the most consecutive seasons.

Question: What honor did he win in 1976, his worst season of the decade?

VIDA ROCHELLE BLUE, JR.
Born: July 28, 1949, Mansfield, Louisiana
Ht. 6'0"; wt. 190 lbs.
Bats right and left, throws left

a. He scored 35 points for his high school basketball team in their state championship.
b. He won both the Cy Young Award and the MVP in his first full year in the AL.
c. In 1979, he led the Giants in wins, innings, complete games, and strikeouts.
d. His 1.82 ERA in 1971 led the AL.
e. His 18 wins in 1978 tied him with Juan Marichal for the most Giant wins in a season in the 1970s.
f. He is the only pitcher in history to start All-Star games for each league.
g. In his last year with Oakland, he lost more games than he had won the year before.
h. He is eighth on the NL list of lifetime shutouts and seventeenth on the list of lifetime shutouts for both leagues combined.

Question: He has the opportunity to win 100 games in each league, a feat accomplished by only three pitchers in history. Who is the one active player to win 100 in each league?

BOBBY LEE BONDS
Born: March 15, 1946, Riverside, California
Ht. 6'1"; wt. 190 lbs.
Bats and throws right

a. In high school, he was the long-jump champion of the state of California.
b. Just prior to his call-up by the Giants, he had 47 RBIs and was hitting .370 in just 60 games with Phoenix.
c. He was the first rookie in the twentieth century to hit a grand slam home run in his first major-league game.
d. In 1973, he became the first player in history to hit 40 home runs and steal 40 bases in the same season.
e. In 1978, he became the first player in history to hit 30 or more home runs and steal 30 or more bases in the same season five times.

f. By the end of the seventies, he had the highest combined total of home runs plus stolen bases, lifetime, of all active players who had hit at least 100 home runs and stolen at least 100 bases.
g. He holds the record for most strikeouts in one season for the San Francisco Giants, the New York Yankees, and the Cleveland Indians.
h. He stole more bases in his career than any other active player.

Question: What does he have in common with Bobby Murcer and Mickey Rivers, in addition to the fact that all three were Yankee outfielders?

LAWRENCE ROBERT (LARRY) BOWA
Born: December 6, 1945, Sacramento, California
Ht. 5'10"; wt. 155 lbs.
Bats both, throws right

a. His father managed the Washington Senators from 1943 through 1947.
b. The Phillies acquired him from the Dodgers' organization.
c. No shortstop who played in 1,000 or more games had a higher fielding percentage.
d. He played in more games than any shortstop in Phillies' history.
e. He led the league in fielding for a shortstop five times in the 1970s, tying an NL record.
f. He stole over 250 bases in the seventies.
g. No shortstop who played in 150 or more games ever made fewer errors in one season than Bowa.
h. He and Dave Cash turned more double plays than any other combo in the 1970s.

Question: Only two other players with 500 or more at-bats went through 1979 without hitting a home run. Can you name them?

GEORGE HOWARD BRETT
Born: May 15, 1953, Glendale, West Virginia
Ht. 6'0"; wt. 200 lbs.
Bats left, throws right

a. He worked on the family farm and did not play high school baseball.
b. He is Ken Brett's younger brother.

c. He is the only Royal in history to hit over .300 three seasons in a row.
d. In 1979, he became only the second player in the AL to hit 20 or more doubles, triples, and home runs in one season.
e. The unique combination of league championships for hits (three times), batting, total bases (twice), doubles (three times), and triples (three times) that he has achieved was never before matched by any player in either league.
f. He has never had 100 RBIs in a season.
g. He and Ty Cobb are the only AL players to ever lead the league in both hits and triples in the same season three times.
h. He has never played a complete season in the major leagues in which he hit under .300.

Question: He and Rod Carew are touted as the most likely players to hit .400, a feat last accomplished by Ted Williams in 1941. Who are the other seven players who have hit .400 in one season in the twentieth century?

LOUIS CLARK (LOU) BROCK
Born: June 18, 1939, El Dorado, Arkansas
Ht. 5'11½"; wt. 172 lbs.
Bats and throws left

a. The Cardinals signed him directly out of high school.
b. Ty Cobb was the only other player in history to have stolen over 100 bases in one season when Brock set his record of 118 in 1974.
c. He was the first player in history to have 20 or more home runs and 50 or more steals in the same year.
d. In 1974, Brock and Bake McBride set a new major-league record for most stolen bases by two members of the same team.
e. He played out the 1979 season, his last, in order to pass Ty Cobb's stolen base record.
f. Only Phil Rizzuto stole more bases in total World Series games than Brock did.
g. Brock and Pete Rose entered the 3,000-hit club in 1979.
h. He has the highest batting average in World Series play, of all the players who appeared in 20 or more games.

Question: The Cubs thought that they had made a great deal with the Cardinals for Brock, obtaining two previous 20-game winners. Who were they, and how did they do?

DAGOBERTO BLANCO (BERT) CAMPANERIS

Born: March 9, 1942, Matanzas, Cuba
Ht. 5'10"; wt. 160 lbs.
Bats and throws right

a. Before becoming a shortstop, he regularly played as an outfielder.
b. He has stolen more bases in his career than Omar Moreno, Mickey Rivers, and Pete Rose combined.
c. He has led both the AL and the NL in stolen bases in different seasons.
d. He has never hit more than five home runs in one season.
e. Although he played in 19 games, he never stole a base in the World Series.
f. Although he played in six games, he never stole a base in an All-Star game.
g. He has stolen more bases in his career than any other active player in either league.
h. At the end of the 1970s, he was still more than 300 stolen bases away from Lou Brock's record.

Question: California obtained him by trading away a man whom many regarded as the best regular utility infielder in the AL. Who was that two-time All-Star?

RODNEY CLINE (ROD) CAREW

Born: October 1, 1945, Gatun, Panama Canal Zone
Ht. 6'0"; wt. 182 lbs.
Bats left, throws right

a. He was first discovered playing in the Little League World Series.
b. He spent the first five years of his career as a center fielder.
c. He was Rookie of the Year in 1967 and AL MVP only three years later.
d. He has won seven batting championships, six of them in the 1970s.

e. In the 1970s, he averaged more than 25 stolen bases a season but fewer than 70 RBIs.
f. In 1979, he joined the 3,000-hit club.
g. He was California's number one pick in the spring 1979 reentry draft.
h. 1979 was the best year of his career.

Question: Who are the four Hall of Famers who have equaled or surpassed Carew's record of career batting titles?

STEVEN NORMAN (STEVE) CARLTON

Born: December 22, 1944, Miami, Florida
Ht. 6'5"; wt. 219 lbs.
Bats and throws left

a. He reads widely in psychology and Eastern philosophy.
b. He won more games and struck out more batters than any other left-hander in the last decade.
c. He won 20 or more games four times in the 1970s.
d. He is tenth on the all-time strikeout list.
e. He has pitched five one-hitters, two in 1979, and holds the modern NL record.
f. He won the Cy Young Award in 1972 and 1977, and he also led the major leagues in wins those years.
g. He abstains completely from alcoholic beverages.
h. At the beginning of the 1980 season, he was only 500 strikeouts short of Walter Johnson's all-time record.

Question: Only three pitchers who were still active at the beginning of the 1980 season had won more games and also had struck out more batters. How many can you name?

CESAR CEDENO

Born: February 25, 1951, Santo Domingo, Dominican Republic
Ht. 6'2"; wt. 195 lbs.
Bats and throws right

a. Of all active players with at least 100 home runs and 100 stolen bases, only three have a higher combined total of home runs and stolen bases than Cedeno has.
b. He was the first man in baseball history to steal 50 or more bases and hit 20 or more home runs, in the same season, three times.

c. Only nine active players have stolen more bases in their career than Cedeno has.
d. He played under two Astro managers.
e. He holds the season and career records for Houston for most stolen bases.
f. In 1972, he set or tied season records for Houston which still stood at the end of the 1970s: most total bases, most extra-base hits, and highest slugging average.
g. He won five Gold Gloves in the 1970s.
h. He has never stolen home.

Question: Cedeno is second on the all-time Houston Astro list for most at-bats, runs, home runs, and total bases. Who is first in all these categories?

CARROLL CHRISTOPHER (CHRIS) CHAMBLISS

Born: December 26, 1948, Dayton, Ohio
Ht. 6'1"; wt. 195 lbs.
Bats left, throws right

a. In 1970, he was the American Association Rookie of the Year and the first rookie ever to win a class-AAA batting title.
b. He was Rookie of the Year again in 1971 and was Cleveland's first player to win that award.
c. His father was a professional football player.
d. In his one year at UCLA, he set new records for most home runs and RBIs.
e. He led all Tribe regulars in batting in 1972 and 1973.
f. By the end of the seventies, he had made the list of the all-time top 50 players with the most lifetime hits.
g. He was traded from the Yankees to the Royals to the Braves in a little over a month.
h. He has never had more than 100 RBIs.

Question: Who were the two players, an infielder and a pitcher, who were traded with Chambliss from the Yankees?

ROBERTO WALKER (BOB) CLEMENTE

Born: August 18, 1934, Carolina, Puerto Rico
Ht. 5'11"; wt. 185 lbs.
Bats and throws right

a. Many feel that he would have been on the 1956 Olympic squad had he not been playing professional baseball.
b. The $10,000 bonus paid to Clemente by the Dodgers was the second-largest bonus ever paid to a Latin American ballplayer, Juan Marichal receiving the highest.
c. At 19, he was moved directly to Montreal, the Dodgers' Triple-A club.
d. The Dodgers sold him to the Pittsburgh Pirates.
e. When he was named MVP of the 1971 World Series, it was the second time he was given this honor.
f. He led the NL in hitting four times.
g. He won the NL MVP only once, but he won by an overwhelming margin.
h. He never hit over .310 in the 1970s.

Question: Why do many regard his last major-league hit as the most memorable?

DAVID ISMAEL (DAVE) CONCEPCION
Born: June 17, 1948, Aragua, Venezuela
Ht. 6'1"; wt. 180 lbs.
Bats and throws right

a. He languished in the minors for six years before coming up to the Reds.
b. Only seven active players have stolen more bases in their lifetimes than he has.
c. He has stolen more bases than any other active Red.
d. Only Belanger, Bowa, and Campaneris placed higher in *Baseball Magazine*'s voting for the shortstop of the decade.
e. He has never hit over .300.
f. Throughout the 1970s, he averaged more than 50 RBIs a season.
g. He was the World Series MVP in 1976.
h. He and Larry Bowa tied for the NL lead in double plays in 1979.

Question: The greatest honor of Concepcion's career occurred in 1977, when he was presented with the Roberto Clemente Award. What is this award for?

DWIGHT MICHAEL (DEWEY) EVANS
Born: November 3, 1951, Santa Monica, California
Ht. 6'3"; wt. 205 lbs.
Bats and throws right

a. In 1972, he won the MVP award of the International League.
b. The Red Sox acquired him from the Oakland A's.
c. He has won three Gold Gloves in his seven full years with Boston.
d. In 1979, he had a higher slugging percentage than Yaz.
e. Of his 21 home runs in 1979, the most memorable was his grand slam at Yankee Stadium on September 3.
f. He led the AL in assists in 1979.
g. He led all AL outfielders in double plays in 1975 and 1979.
h. He hit .375 as a DH in 1978 and 1979.

Question: Evans, Rice, and Lynn are regarded by many as the best outfield in baseball. Did they make more or fewer than 15 errors among them in 1979? Did they hit more or fewer than 100 home runs? Did they have more or fewer than 300 RBIs? Did they steal more or fewer than 30 bases?

ROLAND GLEN (ROLLIE) FINGERS
Born: August 25, 1946, Steubenville, Ohio
Ht. 6'4"; wt. 190 lbs.
Bats and throws right

a. He has never struck out 100 or more batters in one season.
b. In the 1970s, he lost more games than he won.
c. He has saved more World Series games than any other pitcher in history.
d. Although he is the most consistent relief pitcher of the 1970s, he has never led the league in saves in any one season.
e. Only Sparky Lyle saved more games in the 1970s.
f. He set the record for most appearances in a season as a relief pitcher twice during the 1970s.
g. He holds the World Series record for most relief appearances in his career.
h. He pitched in more games in the decade than any other relief pitcher in baseball.

Question: In three seasons with the Padres, Fingers has 85 saves. Who is the pitcher for whom he has most often preserved the win?

CARLTON ERNEST (PUDGE) FISK
Born: December 26, 1947, Bellows Falls, Vermont
Ht. 6'2"; wt. 220 lbs.
Bats and throws right

a. He was Rookie of the Year in 1972.
b. He was MVP in baseball, basketball, and soccer in high school.
c. He has been named starting catcher in four All-Star games.
d. He has caught more games than any other Red Sox player.
e. New York Giants punter Dave Jennings is his cousin.
f. He has played in no fewer than 110 games each season he has been with the Red Sox.
g. He beat Mickey Cochrane's record of most doubles in a season by a catcher.
h. In 1977, he tied the major-league record of only four passed balls in 151 games.

Question: In 1977, he became the fifth catcher in history to score 100 runs and drive in 100 runs in the same year. How many of the others can you name?

MICHAEL KENDALL (MIKE) FLANAGAN
Born: December 16, 1951, Manchester, New Hampshire
Ht. 6'0"; wt. 188 lbs.
Bats and throws left

a. He hurt his arm so badly in an American Legion World Series that many believed that his career was finished.
b. He was scouted for the Orioles by his father, a former Red Sox pitcher.
c. He attended Dartmouth on a baseball scholarship.
d. In 1978, he tied for the AL lead for games started.
e. His arm problem popped up again in 1975, and he was almost dropped by the Orioles.
f. He won more games over the period of 1977 through 1979 than did his teammate Jim Palmer.
g. He won more games in 1979 than any other pitcher in the major leagues.

h. In 1979 his ERA just missed being the best in the major leagues by a few percentage points.

Question: His five shutouts in 1979 tied him for the AL lead with two other pitchers. Can you name them?

GEORGE ARTHUR FOSTER

Born: December 21, 1948, Tuscaloosa, Alabama
Ht. 6'1"; wt. 190 lbs.
Bats and throws right

a. He was a draft choice of the Reds.
b. He has hit more grand-slam home runs than any Red in history.
c. In the last four years of the 1970s, he had more total bases than any other player in the major leagues.
d. In the last four years of the 1970s, he hit more home runs and had more RBIs than any other player in the major leagues.
e. He has never hit a home run in the World Series.
f. His RBI and home run totals in 1977 were each higher than those of any other Red in history.
g. In the 1970s, he led the NL in RBIs in consecutive years twice.
h. In the 1970s, he was the only player in the NL to lead the league in home runs, RBIs, total bases, and slugging percentage in the same year.

Question: Who were the two NL players who had higher slugging percentages in 1979?

STEVEN PATRICK (STEVE) GARVEY

Born: December 22, 1948, Tampa, Florida
Ht. 5'10"; wt. 190 lbs.
Bats and throws right

a. His father often drove the Yankee bus during spring training.
b. He played baseball and basketball at Michigan State University.
c. He was obtained in a trade that also involved Davey Lopes.
d. His career has been riddled with injuries.
e. He has hit over .300 each year he has been with the Dodgers.
f. In 1977, his 33 home runs broke Duke Snider's Dodger record for one season.
g. He has more home runs than Jackie Robinson.
h. He was the first man to be named All-Star MVP twice.

Question: Only one active Dodger had hit more home runs than Garvey's 159. Who is that player?

ROBERT (BOB) GIBSON
Born: November 9, 1935, Omaha, Nebraska
Ht. 6'1"; wt. 190 lbs.
Bats and throws right

a. He once played for the Harlem Globetrotters.
b. He starred at baseball, football, basketball, and track at Omaha Technical High School and attended the University of Nebraska on a football scholarship.
c. At the end of the 1970s, only two pitchers had more career strikeouts.
d. In 1968, he had a 22–9 record and deserved both the Cy Young Award and the MVP but he won neither.
e. He once posted the lowest ERA in the history of the NL.
f. He never threw as fast as he could because he was afraid of hurting someone.
g. He won the NL Cy Young Award again in 1971.
h. Whitey Ford is the only man to win more World Series games.

Question: In 1967, Gibson's leg was broken by a batter who had gotten his 2,000th hit the year before. Who was the batter?

RICHARD MICHAEL (GOOSE) GOSSAGE
Born: July 5, 1951, Colorado Springs, Colorado
Ht. 6'3"; wt. 217 lbs.
Bats and throws right

a. In 1971, he was Midwest League Player of the Year as he posted an 18–2 record and an ERA of 1.83.
b. He roomed with Bucky Dent when they were both with the White Sox.
c. He went directly from A ball to the majors, where he proceeded to lose seven games in a row.
d. He was the Fireman of the Year in 1975 and 1978.
e. Only two AL relief pitchers appeared in more games in 1979.
f. In 1977, he set a new Pirate record by appearing in 72 games.
g. In 1976, he was a starting pitcher and compiled a 9–17 record.

h. In the three All-Star games in which he has appeared, he has an ERA of over 20.

Question: He was traded to the Pirates for a minor-league pitcher and a slugger who played out his option and was signed by the Rangers the next year. Who was the slugger?

RONALD AMES (RON) GUIDRY

Born: August 28, 1950, Lafayette, Louisiana
Ht. 5'11"; wt. 160 lbs.
Bats and throws left

a. He struck out more men in one year than any other Yankee.
b. His 13 straight wins in 1978 set a new record for the 1970s.
c. He was the first Yankee to win 20 games in the 1970s.
d. He did not play high school baseball.
e. He was the first unanimous choice for the Cy Young Award.
f. His nine shutouts in 1978 were the most by an AL lefthander since Babe Ruth.
g. He was the first Yankee since Whitey Ford to win the Cy Young Award.
h. In 1979, he led the league in ERA and strikeouts.

Question: When he won 13 straight in 1978, he broke the Yankee record held by the scout who signed him. What was his name?

KEITH HERNANDEZ

Born: October 20, 1953, San Francisco, California
Ht. 6'1"; wt. 185 lbs.
Bats and throws left

a. His father and one brother were also major-league first basemen.
b. He attended San Mateo College, and his family expected him to become a musician.
c. He led Tulsa, an AA team, in hitting in 1974 with a .351 average.
d. He has never hit under .300 since he came up to the Cardinals.
e. He was NL Rookie of the Year in 1977.
f. When he won the NL Batting crown in 1979, he edged out Pete Rose by less than two percentage points.
g. When he tied Willie Stargell for the NL MVP in 1979, he had more first-place votes but Stargell was named on more ballots.
h. His fielding problems are all that keep him from true stardom.

Question: Hernandez was only the second St. Louis Cardinal to win the MVP since Stan Musial won it in 1957. Who was the other player?

JAMES AUGUSTUS (CATFISH) HUNTER
Born: April 8, 1946, Hertford, North Carolina
Ht. 6'0"; wt. 195 lbs.
Bats and throws right

a. He was nicknamed "Catfish" by Charlie Finley.
b. He moved right into AAA ball, where he won 15 games in his first season as an 18-year-old.
c. He threw the AL's first regular-season perfect game in 46 years.
d. No other AL pitcher had as many consecutive wins in the 1970s as Hunter did.
e. He was the only 20-game winner on the World Champion Oakland A's in 1973.
f. When he led the AL in giving up home runs in 1973, almost two-thirds of them came off his first pitch in the ball game.
g. An infamous gopher-ball pitcher, he never led the AL in ERA.
h. He won the Cy Young Award in his last year with Oakland.

Question: How is it that he spent a year with Daytona Beach in the Florida State League, but never appeared in a game?

REGINALD MARTINEZ (REGGIE) JACKSON
Born: May 18, 1946, Wyncote, Pennsylvania
Ht. 6'0"; wt. 200 lbs.
Bats and throws left

a. He ran the hundred-yard dash in 9.7 seconds in high school.
b. He got a baseball and football scholarship to Arizona State, but he did not earn his degree.
c. The Reverend Jesse Jackson is his cousin.
d. He was 25th on the all-time home-run list at the start of the 1980 season.
e. In 1975, he became the only player to homer in all 12 AL parks in one season.
f. He never won the league MVP.
g. He tied Lou Gehrig's record of at least one RBI in eight straight World Series games.

h. He is the second player in history to have 350 home runs and 200 stolen bases, lifetime.

Question: Everyone remembers Reggie's three home runs in the sixth game of the 1977 World Series. Who were the three pitchers who served up the homers? Did anyone else ever hit three home runs in one World Series game?

FERGUSON ARTHUR (FERGIE) JENKINS

Born: December 13, 1943, Chatham, Ontario, Canada
Ht. 6'5"; wt. 210 lbs.
Bats and throws right

a. One of his favorite pastimes was playing ice hockey.
b. He set a new major-league record in 1972, when he posted his sixth straight season of 20 or more wins with the Chicago Cubs.
c. No pitcher won more games in the 1970s than Jenkins.
d. Jenkins has won more games in his career than any other pitcher still active at the end of the 1979 season.
e. At the end of the 1979 season, Jenkins was within one season of surpassing Cy Young's personal lifetime record of strikeouts.
f. He is on the top-ten list of all pitchers in history in career shutouts.
g. In 1974, when he had a 25–12 season with the Rangers, he joined the very exclusive club of pitchers who have won the Cy Young Award in both leagues.
h. Although a very consistent pitcher year after year, he has never tied or led either league in wins in one season.

Question: Boston's trade of Jenkins back to Texas was one of the best deals the Rangers ever made. Who and what did they give up?

THOMAS EDWARD (TOMMY) JOHN

Born: May 22, 1943, Terre Haute, Indiana
Ht. 6'3"; wt. 203 lbs.
Bats right, throws left

a. He was NL Comeback Player of the Year in 1976.
b. He has won 20 games or more five times since he came up with Cleveland in 1963.
c. He was offered dozens of scholarships to college for basketball.
d. His 2.97 ERA was second to Ron Guidry in the AL in 1979.

e. He is 1–1 against the Yankees in World Series play.
f. He won the Cy Young Award in 1977.
g. The Dodgers traded Richie Allen to the White Sox for John.
h. In 1979, he was second in the AL in wins, innings pitched, and complete games.

Question: When he and Jerry Koosman won 20 games in the AL, they became the seventh and eighth pitchers in history to have 20-game seasons in both leagues. How many of the six men who preceded them can you name?

RANDALL LEO (RANDY) JONES
Born: January 12, 1950, Fullerton, California
Ht. 5'11"; wt. 180 lbs.
Bats and throws right

a. He was a physical education major at UCLA, where his primary interest was running for the track team.
b. Sandy Koufax helped him to develop some of his good pitching habits.
c. He started in the Texas League in 1972, but he was already a strong contender for both the Cy Young Award and the NL MVP by the end of the 1975 season.
d. Two years before he won the Cy Young Award, he led the league in losses.
e. He was the first Padre ever chosen for an All-Star game. Unfortunately, he didn't play in 1975 and he got the loss in 1976.
f. In 1976, he became only the second pitcher in history to win the Cy Young Award after having come in second the year before.
g. He tied Christy Matthewson's NL record of 68 innings without a walk.
h. He has lost more games in the major leagues than he has won.

Question: In 1976, he became the third pitcher from a second-division team to win the Cy Young Award. Can you name the other two, both of whom won in the 1970s?

ALBERT WILLIAM (AL) KALINE
Born: December 19, 1934, Baltimore, Maryland
Ht. 6'1½"; wt. 175 lbs.
Bats and throws right

a. The year he hit .340, he was the youngest man in history to win a batting crown.
b. He once turned down a $100,000 contract because he felt he wasn't worth it.
c. When he finished the 1974 season, only five men had played in more games.
d. At the age of 39, he was the youngest man ever to achieve 3,000 hits.
e. He got his 3,000th hit off Baltimore's Dave McNally.
f. One of the many records he holds is for the most consecutive errorless games by an outfielder.
g. He never played in a World Series in his career.
h. His #6 is the only number to be retired in Tiger history.

Question: Only six other players entered the exclusive 3,000-hit club in the 1970s. How many can you name?

DAVID ARTHUR (DAVE) KINGMAN
Born: December 21, 1948, Pendleton, Oregon
Ht. 6'6"; wt. 210 lbs.
Bats and throws right

a. He was in the outfield twice in the lineups for the Giants on opening days.
b. He had a 9.00 ERA with the Giants.
c. He led the Giants in RBIs and home runs in 1972.
d. He holds the Giants' season record for most home runs.
e. He holds the Mets' season record for most home runs.
f. He once hit home runs in both leagues in the same season.
g. In 1979, he led the NL in home runs and RBIs.
h. He has a lifetime batting average of under .250.

Question: Name the four teams for whom he hit home runs in the 1977 season.

DAVID EARL (DAVEY) LOPES
Born: May 3, 1946, East Providence, Rhode Island
Ht. 5'9"; wt. 170 lbs.
Bats and throws right

a. He attributes his speed and power to a special weight-training program.

b. He was originally signed as an outfielder.
c. He led the league in stolen bases in 1975 and 1976.
d. He set a major-league record by stealing 38 bases in a row without being thrown out.
e. He has hit more home runs in one season than any other NL second baseman in history.
f. He once stole five bases in one game.
g. He is the only Dodger, in the 1970s, to have hit three home runs in one game.
h. He has stolen more bases than any other active player, going into the 1980 season.

Question: He was the fifth team captain in Dodger history. How many of the others can you name?

GREGORY MICHAEL (GREG OR BULL) LUZINSKI
Born: November 22, 1950, Chicago, Illinois
Ht. 6'1"; wt. 225 lbs.
Bats and throws right

a. He has instructed the Phillies to take part of his salary to buy tickets for underprivileged kids.
b. He was the Phillies number-one selection in the June 1968 draft.
c. He led the league in 1979 by being hit by a pitch ten times.
d. He hit .325 with 33 home runs and 120 RBIs when he was named Eastern League Player of the Year at the age of 19.
e. He led the league with 120 RBIs in 1975.
f. He has never been in an All-Star game.
g. He has led the league in strikeouts three times.
h. He hit .309 in 1977 with 99 runs, 39 home runs, and 130 RBIs.

Question: Luzinski came in second in the NL MVP voting in 1977. Who was the winner?

ALBERT WALTER (SPARKY) LYLE
Born: July 22, 1944, Dubois, Pennsylvania
Ht. 6'1"; wt. 195 lbs.
Bats and throws left

a. He was named all-state twice as a high school center fielder.
b. The trade that sent him to the Yankees was one that truly helped both sides.

c. His pet peeve is practical jokers.
d. Ted Williams was the first person to tell Sparky about the slider.
e. He has relieved more games in a row than any other pitcher in history.
f. He saved more games in the 1970s than any other pitcher.
g. In 1977, the year he won the Cy Young Award, he led the league in games and saves.
h. He has won three, saved one, and lost one in postseason play.

Question: He was the first AL reliever to win the Cy Young Award. Who was the NL reliever who won it in 1974?

FREDRIC MICHAEL (FRED) LYNN
Born: February 3, 1952, Chicago, Illinois
Ht. 6'1"; wt. 190 lbs.
Bats and throws left

a. He was AL Rookie of the Year and MVP in 1975.
b. He has played in five All-Star games in a row.
c. He has had a batting average of .300 for five seasons in a row.
d. He was an All-American baseball player at Stanford University.
e. He entered college on a football scholarship.
f. He has had more than 100 RBIs three times with the Red Sox.
g. He led the league in runs in 1976.
h. He has won three Gold Glove awards.

Question: Who was the only other Rookie of the Year for the Red Sox in the 70s?

BILL MADLOCK, JR.
Born: January 12, 1951, Memphis, Tennessee
Ht. 5'11"; wt. 180 lbs.
Bats and throws right

a. A 12-letter man at Decatur Eisenhower High School, he turned down a pro contract to accept one of 150 scholarship offers to play college baseball.
b. He has never scored 100 or more runs in a season.
c. He was the first NL player to win consecutive batting championships since Tommy Davis did so in 1962–63.
d. In six seasons in the NL, he never hit below .300.

e. His .354 batting average in 1975 was the highest of the decade in the NL.
f. He shares the record for most hits in a World Series game.
g. Cubs fans were not happy about trading captain Ron Santo for Madlock.
h. Only three players in the twentieth century scored more runs in one game than Madlock did.

Question: Why did he almost quit baseball in October 1973?

MICHAEL GRANT (MIKE) MARSHALL
Born: January 15, 1943, Adrian, Michigan
Ht. 5'10"; wt. 180 lbs.
Bats and throws right

a. He dropped out of high school to play baseball.
b. He was signed as a starting pitcher, not a reliever.
c. When Houston dealt Marshall to Montreal, it was truly one of those deals that helped both teams.
d. He holds the major-league record for most losses in relief in one season.
e. By the end of the decade, he had appeared in more games than any other pitcher still active.
f. He holds the records for most appearances in one season in each league.
g. He won the Cy Young Award and was named Fireman of the Year in the same year.
h. No relief pitcher in the 1970s won more games in one season than Marshall.

Question: In 1974, as a Dodger, he broke a record held by Elroy Face since 1956. What was that record?

WILLIE LEE McCOVEY
Born: January 10, 1938, Mobile, Alabama
Ht. 6'4"; wt. 225 lbs.
Bats and throws left

a. McCovey was both Rookie of the Year (1959) and MVP (1969). That is a feat no other player matched in the 1970s.
b. Only Lou Gehrig hit more grand-slam home runs in his career than McCovey.

c. At the end of the decade, he had more RBIs than any other active player.
d. He won the NL Comeback Player of the Year Award 18 years after he was named Rookie of the Year.
e. He was the only player in history to hit two home runs in the same inning twice in his career.
f. He and Dick Dietz are the only pair of teammates to hit grand-slam home runs in the same game in the 1970s.
g. He holds the Giants' all-time records for games played, at-bats, home runs, total bases, RBIs, and extra-base hits.
h. He has more career home runs than any other left-handed hitter in NL history.

Question: At the end of the decade, only five active players had more hits than McCovey. How many can you name?

FRANK EDWIN (TUG) McGRAW, JR.
Born: August 30, 1944, Martinez, California
Ht. 6'0"; wt. 180 lbs.
Bats right, throws left

a. He spent his nineteenth birthday in Dublin, showing the local kids how to pitch.
b. In his first appearance in the major leagues, against San Francisco, two men were on base and he walked two men in a row.
c. He turned down many football, baseball, and basketball scholarship offers before signing with the Mets for $15,000.
d. He perfected his screwball on a golf course in Florida.
e. He has more saves than any Met pitcher in history.
f. He holds the Mets all-time record for most saves in a season.
g. Over the last decade, only three pitchers in the major leagues recorded more saves than McGraw.
h. He has never given up a grand-slam home run.

Question: What did Joe Durso, a *New York Times* writer, say about McGraw's trade to the Phillies?

JOE LEONARD MORGAN
Born: September 19, 1943, Bonham, Texas
Ht. 5'7"; wt. 150 lbs.
Bats left, throws right

a. In the 1970s, he never had a 100-RBI season.
b. Teammate Johnny Bench was the only other player in either league to win MVPs in consecutive years.
c. No other active player has stolen as many bases in his career.
d. Of all the active players in either league who have stolen at least 100 bases and hit more than 100 home runs, only Bobby Bonds has a higher combined total.
e. In the 1970s, he averaged 47 stolen bases a season, almost twice as many as Rod Carew.
f. In the 1970s, he never led the league in hitting, but he did once lead the NL in slugging percentage.
g. He was the first player in history to steal 60 or more bases and hit 25 or more home runs in the same season.
h. He *never* led the NL in stolen bases, but, in the 1970s, he led the league in walks twice.

Question: In 1971, the Astros essentially gave up on Morgan and traded him, Jack Billingham, Cesar Geronimo, and others to Cincinnati for three players. Can you name any of these three players?

THURMAN LEE MUNSON
Born: June 7, 1947, Akron, Ohio
Ht. 5'11"; wt. 190 lbs.
Bats and throws right

a. He was the first Yankee captain since Joe DiMaggio.
b. No Yankee catcher ever had a higher fielding percentage than Munson did in 1971.
c. In addition to catching and playing the outfield, he also played first and third as a Yankee.
d. Mickey Mantle is the only player to get more singles in one World Series than Munson.
e. He never had a 100-RBI season.
f. He was the first Yankee MVP since Mickey Mantle.
g. He led the Yankees in batting average twice in the 1970s.
h. In 1970 when he was AL Rookie of the Year, he hit more home runs than any other Yankee rookie in history.

Question: Two other MVPs of the 1970s were also Rookies of the Year. Can you name them?

BOBBY RAY MURCER
Born: May 20, 1946, Oklahoma City, Oklahoma
Ht. 5'11"; wt. 185 lbs.
Bats left, throws right

a. The Cubs lost him to the Yankees in the free-agent draft.
b. He has hit more home runs as a Yankee than any other active Yankee.
c. In high school, he was all-state in football and baseball.
d. In 1972, he led the league offensively in runs and total bases and defensively in putouts and total chances.
e. He once hit four home runs in a row.
f. He first joined the Yankees when he was 19 years old.
g. He was the All-Star shortstop in the Appalachian League.
h. He was traded to the Giants for Bobby Bonds.

Question: He was signed by the same scout who signed Mickey Mantle. What was the name of that scout?

GRAIG (PUFF) NETTLES
Born: August 20, 1944, San Diego, California
Ht. 6'0"; wt. 187 lbs.
Bats left, throws right

a. He was the Indians' Man of the Year in 1971.
b. He received a basketball scholarship to San Diego State.
c. He was Rookie of the Year in the Pacific Coast League.
d. Jim Kaat was involved in the trade of Nettles from Minnesota to Cleveland.
e. He led the Indians in home runs in each of the three seasons he played with them.
f. He has averaged fewer than 135 games a year in the 1970s.
g. He led the league in home runs in 1976 and 1977.
h. He hit 20 or more home runs for seven seasons in a row.

Question: In the 1970s, he was third in the AL in total RBIs. Who were the first two players?

PHILIP HENRY (PHIL) NIEKRO
Born: April 1, 1939, Blaine, Ohio
Ht. 6'1"; wt. 180 lbs.
Bats and throws right

a. He was the youngest man to become a regular starting pitcher in the Braves' history.
b. Younger brother Joe tied him for the NL lead in 1979 with 21, but Phil had fewer losses.
c. Only five pitchers still active in the majors at the end of the decade had more career strikeouts than Niekro.
d. His 44 starts in 1979 were the most in the NL since Grover Cleveland Alexander in 1917.
e. In 1979, he passed Sandy Koufax on the all-time strikeout list.
f. Because of his knuckleball, he has walked almost as many men as he has struck out.
g. He holds the all-time Braves record for wins.
h. In a game against Houston on August 4, 1979, he tied a major-league record by throwing four wild pitches.

Question: Only seven pitchers posted more wins in the 1970s. How many can you name?

PEDRO (TONY) OLIVA

Born: July 20, 1940, Pinar del Rio, Cuba
Ht. 6'2"; wt. 190 lbs.
Bats left, throws right

a. He entered the country on a false passport and he came close to never playing baseball because of it.
b. The Minnesota Twins signed him and assigned him to a Class-AA team.
c. He played winter ball in Puerto Rico and led the league in hitting.
d. He was both the first rookie to lead a major-league in hitting and also the first black to lead the AL.
e. He led the AL in hits five times.
f. His average was never again as high as it was in his rookie year.
g. The year after he won his third, and last, batting championship, he had only ten at-bats.
h. His lifetime batting average is over .300.

Question: Among the many Twins records Oliva holds, one is for the most doubles (329) in his career. Who were his teammates who held the Twins' records for most career singles, triples, and home runs?

AMOS JOSEPH OTIS
Born: April 26, 1947, Mobile, Alabama
Ht. 5'11½"; wt. 169 lbs.
Bats and throws right

a. The Royals signed Otis, a three-letter man, out of Williamson High School in Mobile.
b. His greatest disappointment was in never hitting .300 in the 1970s.
c. In spite of his blinding speed, he has one of the worst ratios of stolen bases to attempts in the major leagues.
d. He is second only to George Brett in almost every Royals career offensive category: at-bats, runs, hits, doubles, RBIs, and home runs.
e. No other major-league player stole more bases in one game in the 1970s.
f. He and Willie Wilson stole more bases between them in one season than any other two teammates in AL history.
g. He is the only Royals player to win the coveted *Sporting News* Gold Glove three times during the 1970s.
h. He is the only AL player during the 1970s to get four walks in one game, four times.

Question: In two consecutive games in 1975, he tied a major-league record that had not been matched since 1912. What was the record, and who set it?

JAMES ALVIN (JIM) PALMER
Born: October 15, 1945, New York City, New York
Ht. 6'3"; wt. 195 lbs.
Bats and throws right

a. He played on the same team as Reggie Jackson at Arizona State University.
b. He was almost waived out of baseball after his disastrous season with Baltimore in 1970.
c. He was originally signed by the Yankees but traded to the Orioles while he was still in the minors.
d. He has never won an All-Star game.
e. He is the only pitcher in the 1970s to win consecutive Cy Young awards.

f. Only Gaylord Perry won more games in the 1970s than did Palmer.
g. Palmer is not on the decade's top-ten list of pitchers with the most strikeouts.
h. He was the youngest pitcher ever to win a complete World Series shutout game.

Question: Palmer was one of four 20-game winners on the 1971 Orioles. Can you name the other three?

DAVID GENE (DAVE) PARKER
Born: June 9, 1951, Jackson, Mississippi
Ht. 6'5"; wt. 230 lbs.
Bats left, throws right

a. He attended a poor rural school in the South that did not have any varsity teams.
b. His knee injury caused him to have such a bad year in 1972 that he almost quit baseball.
c. In 1977, he led the league with a .338 batting average, 215 hits, and 44 doubles, but he was not chosen MVP.
d. In six full seasons with the Pirates, he has never hit below .300.
e. He set a new All-Star record with two assists in the 1979 game.
f. He has never stolen more than ten bases in a season.
g. He was the only player in the NL to win back-to-back batting championships.
h. He led the NL in total bases in 1978 and 1979.

Question: In 1979, he and three other players joined the 36 before them who had four hits in one World Series game. How many of the three can you name?

ATANACIO RIGAL (TONY) PEREZ
Born: May 14, 1942, Camaguey, Cuba
Ht. 6'2"; wt. 210 lbs.
Bats and throws right

a. He has averaged over 22 home runs and 95 RBIs a season during the 1970s.
b. He has played in seven All-Star games and four World Series during his career, all with Cincinnati.

c. During the 1970s, he had more RBIs than any other player in either league.
d. He was MVP of the Pacific Coast League in 1964.
e. He has been named to the All-Star team as both a first baseman and a third baseman.
f. In 1978, he recorded his 300th home run and his 2,000th hit.
g. He has averaged 150 games a year since 1967.
h. The Red Sox signed him in the free-agent reentry draft.

Question: He and Will McEnaney were traded to Montreal for two pitchers. Who were they?

GAYLORD JACKSON PERRY
Born: September 15, 1938, Williamston, North Carolina
Ht. 6'4"; wt. 205 lbs.
Bats and throws right

a. He was all-state in baseball, football, and basketball in high school.
b. He was Pacific Coast League Pitcher of the Year in 1961, and he led the league in ERA in 1962.
c. In 1973, he pitched against his brother Jim, marking the first time in major-league history that brothers faced each other as opposing pitchers.
d. He won the Cy Young Award in both leagues.
e. In the 1970s, he pitched in 369 games and never had an ERA over 3.4.
f. Going into the 1980 season, he had more shutouts in his career than any other active pitcher.
g. He has struck out more than 3,000 batters in his career.
h. He was the first Padre to win a Cy Young Award.

Question: In 1972, Perry (along with Wilbur Wood) became the fourth pitcher in 45 years to be involved in 40 or more decisions. Can you name the other three?

JOHN WESLEY (BOOG) POWELL
Born: August 17, 1941, Lakeland, Florida
Ht. 6'4½"; wt. 230 lbs.
Bats left, throws right

a. He was offered $65,000 by the Milwaukee Braves, but signed for $25,000 with the Baltimore Orioles.
b. His father, a former player in the major leagues, taught him his lifetime hobby of fishing.
c. In 1970, he led both leagues in triples.
d. Former teammate Dean Chance held him virtually hitless over his entire career.
e. He did not hit more home runs in his career than former teammate Frank Robinson.
f. He won the MVP in 1970, unquestionably the best season of his career.
g. In the 1970s, he went over the 100-RBI mark five times.
h. In 1975, he retired from the Orioles rather than take a cut in pay.

Question: Powell had perennial and well-publicized problems with his weight, often ballooning to over 265 pounds. Who made the famous statement about his weight, and what was the statement?

WILLIAM LARRY (WILLIE) RANDOLPH
Born: July 6, 1954, Holly Hill, South Carolina
Ht. 5'11"; wt. 163 lbs.
Bats and throws right

a. He was a three-letter man at Holly Hill high school.
b. He was a first-round draft choice of the Yankees.
c. He has averaged fewer than 125 games a year in his four seasons with the Yankees.
d. He was Rookie of the Year in 1976.
e. He tied for seventh in stolen bases in the AL in 1979.
f. In 1976, he was the first rookie ever listed on the All-Star ballot.
g. He set a record of most assists by a second baseman in the 1977 All-Star game.
h. In 1979, he led the Yankees in games, at-bats, runs, triples, walks, and stolen bases, and he had the second-highest number of hits.

Question: The Yankees gave up a big right-hander who had won 49 games in the three previous seasons in order to get Willie (along with Ken Brett and Dock Ellis). Who was that pitcher, and how did he do with Pittsburgh?

JAMES EDWARD (JIM) RICE
Born: March 8, 1953, Anderson, South Carolina
Ht. 6′2″; wt. 205 lbs.
Bats and throws right

a. He has a .310 career batting average, fifth-best in the 1970s.
b. He was the AL MVP in 1977 and 1978.
c. He won ten letters in high school in baseball, football, basketball, and track.
d. In the years 1976 through 1979, he had a higher total of home runs and RBIs than any other player in the major leagues.
e. He was Minor League Player of the Year in 1974.
f. His 46 home runs in 1978 were the most ever hit by a Red Sox player.
g. In 1978, he was the first player ever to lead either league in home runs, triples, and RBIs.
h. His .552 slugging percentage is the best in Red Sox history.

Question: He is the only active player to have over 400 bases in one season. Only four other players ever had more than his 406 total bases in 1978. How many can you name?

BROOKS CALBERT ROBINSON, JR.
Born: May 18, 1937, Little Rock, Arkansas
Ht. 6′1″; wt. 190 lbs.
Bats and throws right

a. He owns a restaurant in Baltimore called the Golden Arm.
b. He played more games with one team than any other player in the history of the AL.
c. He started 20 consecutive opening-day games with the Orioles.
d. He has the highest fielding percentage of all third basemen who played 100 or more games in the major leagues.
e. He won 16 straight Golden Gloves, a string broken by Graig Nettles.
f. He and Boog Powell were the first two men inducted into the new Orioles Hall of Fame.
g. He holds virtually every Oriole career record, including hits, doubles, triples, home runs, total bases, RBIs, and extra-base hits.
h. In the 1970s, he stole a grand total of 28 bases.

Question: Who gave him the name "Hoover," and what were the circumstances?

FRANK ROBINSON
Born: August 31, 1935, Beaumont, Texas
Ht. 6'1"; wt. 194 lbs.
Bats and throws right

a. He grew up in Oakland and, while in high school, played baseball with Curt Flood, Vada Pinson, and Jesse Gonder, as well as basketball with a youngster named Bill Russell.
b. He was signed by the Cincinnati Reds when he was only 17 and was sent to a Class-C team.
c. He was unanimously selected the NL Rookie of the Year under manager Fred Hutchinson.
d. Only Johnny Bench has hit more home runs as a Cincinnati Red than Robinson. Also, on the all-time Reds list, only Pete Rose had more extra-base hits and runs.
e. He was traded to Baltimore because the Cincinnati general manager observed that Robinson had an "old body" at 30.
f. He is the only player in history to win the MVP in both leagues.
g. He hit home runs in more ball parks than any other player in history.
h. At the end of the decade, only three players in history had hit more home runs in their careers.

Question: On April 8, 1975, opening day at Cleveland's Municipal Stadium, a lady named Rachel threw out the first ball. Why was that particularly significant and historically notable?

PETER EDWARD (PETE) ROSE
Born: April 14, 1941, Cincinnati, Ohio
Ht. 5'11"; wt. 203 lbs.
Bats right and left, throws right

a. His father was a scout for Cincinnati.
b. He has never stolen more than 15 bases in a single season.
c. Only Ty Cobb had 200 or more hits in more seasons than Rose.
d. He has more singles than any other player in NL history.
e. In the 1970s, he hit over .300 nine times.

f. He collected more hits in the 1970s than any other player in either league.
g. He has never had a 100-RBI season.
h. He broke the NL consecutive-game hitting streak set by Wee Willie Keeler.

Question: Only one active player has more total bases in his career than Rose. Who is that player?

LYNN NOLAN RYAN, JR.

Born: January 31, 1947, Refugio, Texas
Ht. 6'2"; wt. 195 lbs.
Bats and throws right

a. He has had only six .500 or more seasons in the 1970s.
b. In the 1970s, he led the AL in strikeouts seven times.
c. By the end of the decade, he was the only pitcher in the twentieth century to have thrown four no-hitters.
d. In the 1970s, he led the AL in bases on balls six times.
e. In the 1970s, he led or tied the AL in shutouts three times and he is within 30 shutouts of Walter Johnson's lifetime record.
f. He has struck out more batters in one season than any other pitcher in either league.
g. In the 1970s, he led both leagues in season strikeouts at least once.
h. His number of career strikeouts is surpassed by only four active pitchers: Gaylord Perry, Steve Carlton, Ferguson Jenkins, and Tom Seaver.

Question: Only four other pitchers in history have had two no-hitters in the same season. Who are they?

MICHAEL JACK (MIKE) SCHMIDT

Born: September 27, 1949, Dayton, Ohio
Ht. 6'2"; wt. 203 lbs.
Bats and throws right

a. He led the American Association League in home runs two seasons in a row before moving up to the Phillies.
b. He was playing AA ball when he was still 17.
c. He is the only player to lead either league in home runs three times in the 1970s.

d. In the last half of the 1970s, he hit more home runs than any other player in either league.
e. In 1979, he won his fourth Gold Glove and was voted "Third Baseman of the Decade" in a *Baseball Magazine* survey.
f. His 45 home runs in 1979 led the NL and set a Phillies' season record.
g. He has had more than 100 runs, RBIs, and bases on balls in one season four times.
h. He was the first Phillie since Dick Allen to be named MVP.

Question: He was named to four All-Star teams in the 1970s, more than any other Phillie. Who was the Phillie who was named three times?

GEORGE THOMAS (TOM) SEAVER
Born: November 17, 1944, Fresno, California
Ht. 6'0"; wt. 200 lbs.
Bats and throws right

a. He was originally signed by the Atlanta Braves.
b. In his first year with the Mets, he was named NL Rookie of the Year and accounted for 26 percent of the team's wins.
c. He won over 100 games in his first five years with the Mets.
d. He won the Cy Young Award twice.
e. In the 1970s, he struck out 200 or more batters ten times.
f. In the 1970s, he led the league in strikeouts five times and ERA three times.
g. In the 1970s, he led the league in complete games four times.
h. Only five active pitchers had more career strikeouts at the end of the 1970s.

Question: Who *are* the two active pitchers with more career strikeouts than Seaver?

DANIEL JOSEPH (RUSTY) STAUB
Born: April 1, 1944, New Orleans, Louisiana
Ht. 6'2"; wt. 205 lbs.
Bats left, throws right

a. Only three players in NL history got more extra-base hits in one game than Staub did.

b. In the only World Series in which he appeared, he had more hits than any other player on either team.
c. No left-hander who played through the entire decade grounded into fewer double plays in his career.
d. He has hit grand-slam home runs in both leagues.
e. He tied the NL record for double plays by an outfielder three times.
f. He has the highest RBI record for one season in Mets history.
g. He has the highest season batting average in Astro history.
h. In 1978, he played in 162 games but had no putouts or assists.

Question: He says that his most memorable game was played in 1973, the day after the season was supposed to have ended. What were the circumstances of that game?

WILVER DORNELL (WILLIE) STARGELL
Born: March 6, 1941, Earlsboro, Oklahoma
Ht. 6'3"; wt. 225 lbs.
Bats and throws left

a. He attended a Catholic mission school, intended primarily for Indians, which did not have any sports facilities.
b. At one time or another, in the minor and major leagues, he played with the Dodgers, Reds, and Cubs organizations.
c. He is second only to Bobby Bonds for the record of most consecutive seasons with 100 or more strikeouts.
d. In the 1970s, he led the NL twice in home runs.
e. Roberto Clemente is the only Pirate in history to have more lifetime home runs, RBIs, or extra-base hits.
f. Of all players still active at the end of the 1979 season, only Willie McCovey had more home runs.
g. In the 1970s, he had only one season in which he had more RBIs than strikeouts.
h. In 1979, he set a new World Series record by getting seven extra-base hits.

Question: He was the co-recipient of two major honors in 1979. Everybody knows what one of them is. Can you name them both?

HOWARD BRUCE SUTTER
Born: January 8, 1953, Lancaster, Pennsylvania
Ht. 6'2"; wt. 190 lbs.
Bats and throws right

a. The Washington Senators drafted him when he was only seventeen.
b. At the end of the decade, he had over 150 saves.
c. He has won two All-Star games.
d. No pitcher has ever saved more games in one season than his 37 in 1979.
e. Tom Seaver is the only NL pitcher to strike out more batters in a row in the seventies.
f. He is one of only three pitchers to strike out the side on nine pitches, in the seventies.
g. He has been named Fireman of the Year and he has won a Cy Young Award but not in the same year.
h. His combination of 43 wins and saves in 1979 was the highest of the decade of all relief pitchers.

Question: Who are the two NL pitchers who share his record of 37 saves in one season?

DONALD HOWARD (DON) SUTTON
Born: April 2, 1945, Clio, Alabama
Ht. 6'1"; wt. 185 lbs.
Bats and throws right

a. He lost 13 games in a row to the Cubs.
b. In 1974, he set Championship Series records for most scoreless innings in a row, most innings pitched, and most strikeouts in a four-game series.
c. He and Sandy Koufax struck out more batters in 1966 than any other two pitchers in history except Koufax and Don Drysdale.
d. He has never won an All-Star game.
e. He averaged fewer than 15 wins a year throughout the 1970s.
f. Only 50 pitchers in major-league history have won more games.
g. He was the starting pitcher for the Dodgers on every opening day from 1972 through 1979.
h. He has struck out more batters than any other Dodger in history.

Question: Only 12 pitchers in major-league history had more shutouts than Sutton had at the end of the seventies. How many shutouts did he have? Who holds the record?

LUIS CLEMENTE TIANT
Born: November 23, 1940, Havana, Cuba
Ht. 5'11"; wt. 187 lbs.
Bats and throws right

a. Many people say that Luis's father was a better pitcher than he was.
b. Just two years after he led the AL with a 1.60 ERA while winning 21 games, he was released by Cleveland and was back in the minors.
c. He is one of the ten pitchers in history to have pitched over 50 career shutouts.
d. He struck out more players in an extra-inning game than any other player in major-league history.
e. He and Sudden Sam McDowell struck out more batters in one season than any other two pitchers on the same team.
f. The Boston fans were very annoyed when George Scott was traded to obtain Tiant.
g. He was the first Red Sox pitcher to win 20 or more games for three years in a row since Cy Young and Bill Dinneen both accomplished that feat in 1904.
h. He had more games in his career in which he struck out ten or more batters than did Don Sutton, Don Drysdale, Lefty Grove, or Vida Blue.

Question: Tiant's nine shutouts in 1968 led the AL and tied him with a former Red Sox pitcher who also led the AL over 50 years earlier. Who was that pitcher?

ROY WHITE
Born: December 27, 1943, Los Angeles, California
Ht. 5'10"; wt. 172 lbs.
Bats left and right, throws right

a. The Yankees signed him in 1962, hoping he could replace the aging Tom Tresh at shortstop.
b. In 1971, he became the first Yankee in history to play a full season without making an error.

c. He stole more bases in his career than any other Yankee.
d. He led the AL in runs in 1976.
e. He played more games with the Yankees than Joe DiMaggio.
f. In 1968, he led or tied the Yankees in batting average, runs, hits, doubles, triples, RBIs, and stolen bases.
g. When he stole 24 bases in 1970, that was the most by a Yankee since 1945.
h. Of players who have hit at least 100 home runs and stolen at least 100 bases, he is on the top-ten all-time list in total.

Question: Only four Yankees have played in more games than White, and they are all in the Hall of Fame. How many can you name?

BILLY LEO WILLIAMS
Born: June 15, 1938, Whisler, Alabama
Ht. 6'1"; wt. 175 lbs.
Bats left, throws right

a. He is on the NL list of the top-ten home-run hitters.
b. He was the first Cub since 1945 to win an NL batting crown.
c. No player in history ever hit more doubles in one game.
d. No player in the 1970s scored more runs in one game.
e. He won the NL batting crown five years after he was NL Rookie of the Year.
f. He holds the all-time Cubs records for home runs, total bases, and extra-base hits.
g. In 1970, he had more hits than Pete Rose.
h. Basically a line-drive hitter, he never hit more than 30 home runs in one season.

Question: He is one of only four players in history to play in over 1,000 consecutive games. One was Lou Gehrig, of course, but name the other two.

WILLIE JAMES WILSON
Born: July 9, 1955, Montgomery, Alabama
Ht. 6'2"; wt. 190 lbs.
Bats right and left, throws right

a. A star in baseball, football, and basketball, many say that he was the best all-around schoolboy athlete in California since Jackie Robinson.

b. He passed up hundreds of offers of football scholarships to sign with the White Sox.
c. He has led three different leagues in stolen bases.
d. He and teammate Amos Otis stole more bases between them than Lou Brock and Bake McBride in Brock's best year.
e. He became a switch-hitter in Little League.
f. In 1979, he was the only man in the major leagues to steal more than 50 bases and hit over .300.
g. He has tried to pattern his career after that of Herb Washington.

Question: He led the AL in 1979 in a category other than stolen bases. His stat in that category was 588.00. What is the category, and what does that stat represent.

CARL MICHAEL YASTRZEMSKI
Born: August 22, 1939, Southampton, New York
Ht. 6'0"; wt. 180 lbs.
Bats left, throws right

a. The Red Sox signed him as a catcher after a year at Notre Dame.
b. Of all players still active at the end of the 1970s only Pete Rose had played in more games, had more RBIs, or had more extra-base hits.
c. He was the last player of the decade to join the 3,000-hit club.
d. He holds the record for the most intentional walks in his career.
e. There have only been four players to have 100 RBIs in a season who were older than him.
f. He is the only player in the 1970s to have a combined total of more than 300 hits and walks in one season.
g. He grounded into more double plays in his career than any other left hander in history.
h. At the end of the 1979 season he had more home runs than any other active player.

Question: Only three other players in history had over 3,000 hits and more than 400 home runs. Can you name the three?

Hank Aaron

True: f (His 3,771 hits are 420 short of Ty Cobb's 4,191 hits. Cobb played one year more than Aaron.); g (Willie McCovey's 520 was the closest to Aaron's 755.); h (This is one he would like to forget, but he did hit into a record 328 double plays in his career.)

False: a (In spite of his many records over many years, he won the NL MVP only once, in 1957. That year he led the league with 44 home runs, 118 runs, and 132 RBIs.); b (He hurt his right ankle in his rookie year, but in his 23-year career, he played in at least 140 games a year for 16 straight years, and only twice did he play in fewer than 120 games.); c (In 1963, Aaron stole 31 bases and hit 44 home runs, but Willie Mays and Bobby Bonds also belong to the 30/30 club.); d (This was the plan of Manager Eddie Mathews, but Commissioner Kuhn ruled against him. He hit number 714 in the first game, sat out the second, and went 0 for 3 in the third. He did break the record at home.); e (Billingham served up the 714th. The dubious honor of pitching the 715th belongs to Al Downing, the former Yankee then with the Dodgers.)

Answer: Bobby Thomson, acquired from the Giants for former bonus baby Johnny Antonelli, broke his leg sliding into second. Infielder Aaron suddenly became an outfielder, and he played in 122 games in his rookie year, 1954. He hit .280 for the season, with 13 homers.

Dick Allen

True: d (In spite of being very unhappy, he led the International League with 33 home runs and 97 RBIs in 145 games. He ended the season with the Phillies.); e (He scored 125 runs, hit 29 home runs, had 352 total bases, 80 extra base hits—all in 1964—and he had a slugging percentage of .632 in 1966; f (His 37 home runs in 1972 still stand as the club record, as does his .603 slugging percentage.); g (Although he never played for Atlanta, he was traded to them from the White Sox. Atlanta then traded him back to the Phillies. In 1972, he played in 54 games and hit .240 with Oakland, the end of a long and sad odyssey.)

False: a (Not only was he not an only child, but brothers Hank and Ron were both major-league ballplayers. Hank played first, second, third, outfield, and even caught one game in his seven-year career.); b (He was AL MVP, but the manager was Chuck Tanner, who came from a neighboring town in western Pennsylvania and who had known Allen since Dick was a youngster.); c (Allen was Rookie of the Year in 1964, fitting in between Pete Rose in 1963 and Joe Morgan in 1965.); h (In 1971, he played in 155 games for the

Dodgers and, in 1972, he played in the first 148 games for the White Sox before being benched with a knee injury.)

Answer: Allen, along with Cookie Rojas and Jerry Johnson, was traded from the Phillies to the Cardinals for Tim McCarver, Joe Hoerner, Byron Browne, and Curt Flood. Flood refused to report, and Arthur J. Goldberg sued on his behalf in federal court, challenging baseball's long-entrenched reserve system.

Don Baylor

True: c (He hit .296 with 36 home runs, and he led the league with 120 runs and 139 RBIs.); d (With Rochester in the International League that year, he hit .327, and had 22 home runs and 107 RBIs.); e (He stole 24, 32, 29, and 32 bases from 1972 through 1975.); h (He has 167 home runs and 240 stolen bases, for a total of 407, as compared to Rose's 154 home runs and 155 stolen bases for a total of 299.)

False: a (Although born in Austin, Texas, he attended Miami-Dade Junior College and Blinn Junior College in Texas.); b (He was the number two pick, but present teammate Bobby Grich was number one.); f (Baylor, along with pitchers Mike Torrez and Paul Mitchell, was traded for Reggie Jackson, Ken Holtzman, and Bill Van Brummel.); g (He hit 25 with Baltimore in 1975, 15 with Oakland in 1976, and 25, 34, and 36 the next three years with California.)

Answer: Ken Singleton was second in voting with 241 points, and George Brett was third with 226 points.

Johnny Bench

True: a (His pitching record was 75–3.); c (He was NL Rookie of the Year in 1968 and MVP in 1970.); d (His 332 surpassed Frank Robinson's record of 324 as a Red.)

False: b (He was chosen second, after Bernie Carbo.); e (Yogi Berra's 358 is the only catcher's mark ahead of his 332.); f (His 1,013 RBIs in the 1970s put him far ahead of his two closest competitors, teammates Tony Perez and Lee May, with 954 and 936 respectively.); g (He never led in all four categories in the same year.); h (No, he *tied* Bill Dickey's record in 1979.)

Answer: After a 1976 season of hitting .234 with only 16 home runs, he went on to win the World Series MVP with a .533 average and 6 RBIs.

Vida Blue

True: b (The year was 1971. Although he did win 2 and lose 0 for Oakland in 1970, he also posted a 12–3 record with Iowa.); c (He had 14 wins, 237 innings, 10 complete games, and 138 strikeouts.); d; f (He started the 1975 game when he was with Oakland and the 1978 game when he was with San Francisco.); g (He won 18 in 1976 and lost 19 in 1977.); h

False: a (However, he did lead the DeSoto High School football team to a conference championship and, as quarterback, he threw 35 touchdowns in 1967. Jesse Hudson, who pitched two innings for the Mets in 1969, caught 17 of those touchdown passes.); e (Gaylord Perry led the league with 23 wins in 1970, and Ron Bryant led the league in 1973 with 24 wins.)

Answer: Gaylord Perry is the only active pitcher to have won 100 in each league. Cy Young and Jim Bunning were the other two pitchers.

Bobby Bonds

True: a (It was when he was a senior at Riverside Polytechnic High School.); b; c (On June 25, 1968, his third at-bat and his first hit was a grand slammer off the Dodgers' John Purdin.); e (Willie Mays did it twice.); g (He struck out 189 times with the Giants in 1970, 137 times with the Yankees in 1975, and 135 times with the Indians in 1979.)

False: d (He stole 43 bases, but his home-run tally fell one short at 39.); f (His total of 761 was second to Joe Morgan's total of 814.); h (His 441 stolen bases at the end of the 1970s were third to Bert Campaneris's 628 and Joe Morgan's 601.)

Answer: The Yankees traded Murcer to the Giants for Bonds, and they traded Bonds to the Angels for Rivers (and Figueroa).

Larry Bowa

True: c (He has the best fielding average, .982, of all shortstops.); d (He is almost 200 games ahead of Mickey Doolan (1905–1913) and almost 600 ahead of Granny Hamner (1944–1959).); e (He led the league in 1971, 1972, 1974, 1978, and 1979.); f (He stole 251 bases in ten years with the Phillies.); h (They turned 245 double plays in 1974.)

False: a (The Senators' manager in those years was Ossie Bluege. Bowa's father, Paul, was a minor-league manager and player.); b (He was signed as a free agent in 1965 and assigned to Spartanburg in the Western Carolinas League.); g (Bowa's 9 errors in 1972 was an NL record but Ed Brinkman made only 7 errors in 1974.)

Answer: Ozzie Smith of the Padres and Craig Reynolds of the Astros.

George Brett

True: b (Ken was born in September 1948.); d (Jeff Heath of Cleveland was the only other AL player to accomplish this, in 1941.); g (Brett did it in 1975, 1976, and 1979; Cobb did it in 1908, 1911, and 1917.)

False: a (He grew up in El Segundo, California, where his major interests were baseball and surfing.); c (Hal McRae hit .310, .306, and .332 in 1974, 1975, and 1976.); e (Ty Cobb and Lou Gehrig both achieved this unique combination before him.); f (1979 was the first year he had over 100 RBIs, 107 to be precise.); h (He "slumped" to .294 in 1978.)

Answer: They are: Bill Terry (.401 in 1930), Rogers Hornsby (.403 in 1925, .424 in 1924, and .401 in 1922), Harry Heilman (.403 in 1923), George Sisler (.420 in 1922, .407 in 1920), Ty Cobb (.401 in 1922, .410 in 1912, .420 in 1911), Joe Jackson (.408 in 1911), and Napoleon Lajoie (.422 in 1901).

Lou Brock

True: c (He stole 52 bases and hit 21 home runs in 1967. By the end of the decade, Cesar Cedeno and Joe Morgan had joined him in that exclusive club.); d (Their total of 148 erased the 1913 record of 137 of Clyde Milan and Danny Moeller of the Washington Senators.); h (He hit .391, 34 for 87, in 21 games, a World Series record.)

False: a (He attended Southern University in Baton Rouge and signed with the Cubs for a reported $30,000 in 1961.); b (Maury Wills had stolen 104 bases in 1962. The most bases Cobb ever stole in one season was 96, in 1915.); e (He stole his 892nd and 893rd bases on August 29, 1977, in San Diego.); f (The Scooter stole 10 bases in nine World Series, but Brock stole 14 in three World Series, tying Eddie Collins's record.); g (Brock got his 3,000th hit on August 13, 1979, against the Cubs, but Rose got his 3,000th hit in 1978. Carl Yastrzemski was the other player to join the 3,000-hit club in 1979, just one month after Brock.)

Answer: Ernie Broglio could achieve only a 7–19 record with Chicago before retiring, and Bobby Shantz won none and lost one before moving to the Phillies and retiring the same year.

Bert Campaneris

True: b (Moreno's 217, Rivers's 226, and Rose's 155 add up to 598, compared to Campaneris's record of 628.); f; g (The closest is Joe Morgan with 601.); h (He was 310 behind Brock's 938 bases.)

False: a (He played first base, third base, catcher, and he even pitched on rare occasions.); c (He never played in the NL.); d (He hit more than five home runs in several seasons, including 1970, when he hit 22 with Oakland.); e (He stole five bases in World Series play, including the three he stole against the Mets in 1973.)

Answer: The Texas Rangers traded him to California in May 1979 for Dave Chalk, who had averaged over 141 games a season for the Angels. Campaneris was hurt several times in 1979 and played in only 85 games.

Rod Carew

True: d; e (He stole 253 bases but had only 628 RBIs.)

False: a (He moved to New York when he was 15 and the Twins found him playing sandlot ball in the shadow of Yankee Stadium.); b (He was primarily a second baseman until he moved to first base in 1976.); c (He was not voted MVP until 1977.); f (He finished 1979 with 2,215 hits.); g (He forced a trade by announcing that he would become a free agent rather than continue playing for Calvin Griffith, the Twins' owner. He went to California for Ken Landreaux, Dave Engle, Paul Hartzell, and Brad Havens.); h (1979 was one of his worst seasons, as injuries took him out of the lineup for almost seven weeks. He "only" hit .318, played in 110 games, had 409 at bats and 130 hits.)

Answer: Ty Cobb, with 12 batting titles, and Honus Wagner, with 8, surpass him, and Rogers Hornsby and Stan Musial, each with 7, tie him.

Steve Carlton

True: a; b; c (He won 20 in 1971, 27 in 1972, 20 in 1976, and 23 in 1977.); d (He had struck out 2,683 at the beginning of the 1980 season.); f

False: e (He is tied with Don Sutton, Tom Seaver, Jim Maloney, Grover Cleveland Alexander, and Mordecai Brown.); g (He enjoys wine a great deal and recently spent some of his off-season in the wine fields of Burgundy.); h (He was some 825 short of Johnson's 3,508 strikeouts.)

Answer: The three pitchers were Gaylord Perry, Tom Seaver, and Ferguson Jenkins.

Cesar Cedeno

True: a (Only Morgan, Bonds, and Jackson top him on this list.); b (He not only performed this remarkable feat, but he did it in consecutive years: 1972, 1973, and 1974.); e (He stole 61 bases in 1977 and 427 in his career.); f (He had 300 total bases, 69 extra-base hits, and a slugging average of .537.); g

False: c (Only Bert Campaneris, Joe Morgan, and Bobby Bonds have stolen more bases in their lifetimes.); d (He played under Harry Walker, Leo Durocher, Preston Gomez, and Bill Virdon.); h (He has stolen home five times.)

Answer: Jimmy Wynn leads the Astros in all these career categories. "The Toy Cannon" played with Houston from 1963 to 1973 and then had two excellent years with the Dodgers before playing with the Braves and the Yankees.

Chris Chambliss

True: a; d; e; h (His best year was 1976, when he had 96 RBIs.)

False: b (Herb Score was Cleveland's Rookie of the Year in 1955.); c (His father was a career navy chaplain.); f (His 1,382 hits put him 68th on the list. The highest active player on the list is Pete

Rose, who is sixth, with 3,372 hits.); g (The Yankees traded him to the Blue Jays, not the Royals.)

Answer: The two promising prospects whom the Yankees gave up were Damaso Garcia and Paul Mirabella. In exchange, the Yankees got Rick Cerone, Tom Underwood, and Tom Wilborn.

Roberto Clemente

True: a (He had outstanding marks in the hop, skip, and jump event, today called the triple jump.); c (He joined former pitching ace Joe Black and future stars Sandy Amoros and Gino Cimoli.); f (He led with .351 in 1961, .329 in 1964 and 1965, and .357 in 1967. Only four men—Honus Wagner, Rogers Hornsby, Paul Waner, and Stan Musial—in NL history had ever won more than two batting titles.)

False: b (Marichal received only $500. Incidentally, the Milwaukee Braves offered Clemente $30,000 later the same day, but his mother felt that he had given his word to the Dodgers.); d (The Dodgers tried to hide him in the minor leagues, many say because of a color quota on the Brooklyn team, but the Pirates still made him the number-one draft choice.); e (He was MVP in the 1971 Series, hitting .414 with two home runs. He felt that he should have won in 1960 also, but Mazeroski's homer against the Yankees in the bottom of the ninth in the seventh game stole the headlines.); g (In 1966, he just edged out Sandy Koufax by 218 votes to 208. Clemente hit .317 with 29 home runs and 119 RBIs. He also had 202 hits and 105 runs. Koufax had a pretty fair year with 27 wins, 27 complete games, 317 strikeouts, and an ERA of 1.73.); h (He hit .352 in 1970, .341 in 1971, and .312 in 1972. His lifetime batting average over 18 seasons was .317.)

Answer: His double off Jon Matlack was his 3,000th hit, making him only the eleventh player to hit that mark. His plane crashed on New Year's Eve 1972, while on a mercy mission to the Nicaraguan earthquake victims.

Dave Concepcion

True: f (He had 529 RBIs in the 1970s.)

False: a (He was signed by Cincinnati as a free agent and assigned to Tampa in the Florida State League, where he played in

1968. He split the 1969 season between Asheville and Indianapolis, and he played 101 games with Cincinnati in 1970.); b (His 220 stolen bases put him seventeenth on the list of active players.); c (Joe Morgan has stolen 406 bases.); d (He finished well ahead of all of them.); e (He hit .301 in 1978.); g (Johnny Bench was World Series MVP in 1976.); h (Garry Templeton tied him for the lead with 102 double plays. Eight players in all had more than Bowa's 80.)

Answer: The award is for Latin America's top baseball player. Concepcion respected Clemente as the greatest player he had ever seen.

Dewey Evans

True: a (He hit .300 and drove in 95 runs with Louisville.); c; d (He had a .456 slugging average compared to Yaz's .450.); h

False: b (He was the number-five draft pick in the June 1969 draft.); e (He has never hit a grand slam.); f (Bob Bailor's 16 assists edged him out.); g (He did lead the league in 1975 with eight double plays. In 1979, he made five dps, tying him with Amos Otis and just behind Richie Zisk's six.)

Answer: Among them, they committed 13 errors, hit 99 home runs, had 310 RBIs, and stole 30 bases in 1979.

Rollie Fingers

True: b (His win-loss record for the decade is 64–75.); c (His six saves in the 1972, 1973, and 1974 World Series with the Oakland A's, set a new record.); g (His 16 appearances in relief top all pitchers.); h (He appeared in 640 games in the 1970s.)

False: a (He struck out over 100 batters five times in the 1970s.); d (He led the NL in saves with 35 in 1977 and 37 in 1978. The latter tied an NL record.); e (Fingers saved 209 games during the regular season in the 1970s, 19 more than Lyle. As a matter of fact, he was the only man to save more than 200 games in the decade.); f (Actually he held the record three times, twice with Oakland and once with San Diego. He appeared in 76 games in 1974, 75 games in 1975, and 78 games in 1977.)

Answer: Fingers has saved 17 games out of the 30 that Randy Jones won in 1977, 1978, and 1979.

Pudge Fisk

True: a; b; c; e; h

False: d (At the end of the 1979 season, he was still 93 games short of Sammy White's 967 games.); f (He was on the disabled list in both 1974 and 1975, and elbow problems allowed him to play only 91 games in 1979.); g (He hit 39 doubles in 1978, but Cochrane still holds the record with 42 doubles in 1930.)

Answer: The four catchers who held that mark before him are Mickey Cochrane ('32), Yogi Berra ('50), Roy Campanella ('53), and Johnny Bench ('74).

Mike Flanagan

True: a (He had to finish the game in center field and, as a matter of fact, Houston was eager to sign him as an outfielder because of his excellent hitting.); d (He started 40 games and had a 19–15 record.); f (Flanagan's three years of 15, 19, and 23 wins add up to more than do Palmer's records of 20, 21, and 10 wins.); g (He won 23 games in 1979. This was two more than Tommy John, his closest competitor, who had 21 wins.)

False: b (His father did handle the negotiations, but he was scouted by John Stokoe.); c (He played with Dick Berquist at the University of Massachusetts.); e (Far from it. He led the International League with a .765 winning percentage and a 13–4 record.); h (His 3.08 ERA was well behind Ron Guidry's 2.78. Tommy John and Dennis Eckersley also had better ERAs in the AL. Nine pitchers in the NL also had better ERAs.)

Answer: The other two pitchers with five shutouts in 1979 were the Angels' Nolan Ryan and Kansas City's Dennis Leonard.

George Foster

True: d (He had 151 home runs and 487 RBIs, two more home runs and nine more RBIs than his closest competitor, Jim Rice.); e (He had 14 hits for 43 at-bats, but no home runs.); f (His 52 home runs and 149 RBIs are more than any other Red in history. They surpass Ted Kluszewski's 49 home runs in 1954 and Johnny Bench's 148 RBIs, also in 1977.); h (He led the NL in these four categories in 1977.)

False: a (In perhaps the worst trade of the 1970s, the Giants dealt him to Cincinnati for Frank Duffy and Vern Geishert in 1971.); b (Johnny Bench has two more than Foster's seven grand slams.); c (Foster's total of 1,263 bases is surpassed by Jim Rice's 1,437.); g (But he was the only player in the NL to lead the league in RBIs three seasons in a row.)

Answer: Dave Kingman's .613 and Mike Schmidt's .564 were higher than Foster's .561.

Steve Garvey

True: g; h

False: a (His father drove the Dodger bus for Greyhound.); b (He played football, not basketball, and he tackled the great O. J. Simpson twice when he played against USC.); c (He was the Dodgers' number-one selection in 1978 in the special phase of the free-agent draft.); d (Far from it. He is one of baseball's most durable players, and he had played in 672 consecutive games going into the 1980 season.); e (He fell below .300 in 1971, 1972, and 1977.); f (Snider hit 40 in 1957, but Garvey's 33 was the most since then.)

Answer: Ron Cey had hit 163 going into the 1980 season.

Bob Gibson

True: a (He played with them during his first year out of college.); c (His 3,117 strikeouts were surpassed only by Walter Johnson's 3,508 and Gaylord Perry's 3,141.); h (Ford had a 10–8 record over eleven World Series, while Gibson posted a 7–2 record in three World Series. Red Ruffing and Allie Reynolds also have 7–2 records. Gibson's seven wins were, unbelievably, not only consecutive but also complete games.)

False: b (He was a great high school athlete but he believes Nebraska turned him down because he was black. He went to Creighton University, where he integrated the basketball and baseball teams.); d (He won both. By the way, he also had a 1.12 ERA, 268 strikeouts, and 13 shutouts, all league leaders.); e (His 1.12 [1968] was second only to Three Finger Brown's 1.04 in 1906.); f (He always threw his hardest, and he was one of the most threatening, intimidating pitchers of his day.); g (Ferguson Jenkins won the Cy Young Award in 1971. Gibson won in 1968 and 1970.)

Answer: Roberto Clemente smashed a line drive off Gibson's shin, breaking a bone. Gibson picked up the ball, threw Clemente out, and faced two more batters before leaving the game.

Goose Gossage

True: a; b; d (He had 26 saves and a 9–8 record with a 1.84 ERA with Chicago in 1975, and 27 saves and a 10–11 record with a 2.01 ERA with New York in 1978.); f (He figured in 37 of their wins by saving 26 and winning 11 with a 1.62 ERA.); g; h (He pitched three innings and gave up seven earned runs on six hits and two walks for an ERA of 21.00.)

False: c (He *won* seven in a row.); e (He was sixth in appearances with 18 as he missed 12 weeks of the season due to an operation on his thumb after a clubhouse scuffle.)

Answer: It was outfielder Richie Zisk, who hit .290 with Chicago while hitting 30 home runs and knocking in 101 RBIs. The pitcher, by the way, was Silvio Martinez, who pitched 21 innings in ten games with Chicago, was later traded to the Cardinals, and was sent down to Springfield for a while.

Ron Guidry

True: a (His 248 in 1978 surpassed Jack Chesbro's 239 in 1904.); d (His school had no baseball team, but he did star in track.); f

False: b (Steve Carlton won 15 in a row in 1972 and Gaylord Perry did the same in 1974.); c (He was the third: Fritz Peterson won 20 in 1970 and Catfish Hunter won 23 in 1975.); e (Denny McLain was the first, in 1968.); g (Sparky Lyle won it in 1977.); h (His 2.78 ERA was tops, but his 201 strikeouts were second to Nolan Ryan's 223.)

Answer: The scout was Atley Donald, a Yankee from 1938 to 1945, who amassed a record of 65 wins and 33 losses. Interestingly, he never won more than 13 games in any year.

Keith Hernandez

True: c

False: a (They both played in the Cardinal organization, but neither made it to the major leagues.); b (He was groomed to be a major-league ballplayer since he was seven years old, and the Cardinals signed him right out of high school.); d (1979 was the first year he did hit over .300.); e (Andre Dawson was Rookie of the Year in 1977.); f (He hit .344 to Rose's .331.); g (Just the reverse is true.); h (He is an excellent fielder and was named to *The Sporting News* All-Star fielding team in 1978 and 1979.)

Answer: Joe Torre won the MVP in 1971, when he led the league with a .363 batting average, 137 RBIs, and 230 hits.

Catfish Hunter

True: c (He no-hit the Minnesota Twins on May 8, 1968, retiring all 27 batters and winning 4–0, while striking out 11. He also drove in all four runs himself.); f (Of the 39 home runs, 22 were off his first pitch.); h (In 1974, he also led the league with 25 wins, striking out 143 while walking only 45.)

False: a (*Sporting News* says so, but *Baseball Digest* has Hunter telling the story that he got the nickname when he ran away from home at age six to go for catfish. Take your choice.); b (He never pitched an inning of minor-league ball.); d (Hunter's 13 wins in a row with Oakland in 1973 are tied by Ron Guidry for New York in 1978 and Dave McNally for Baltimore in 1971. All are surpassed by Gaylord Perry's 15 for Cleveland in 1974.); e (There were also Ken Holtzman, who won 21, and Vida Blue, who won 20.); g (His 2.49 ERA in 1974 with Oakland did lead the league.)

Answer: He was on the disabled list, recovering from a hunting accident in which his brother blew off a toe with a shotgun.

Reggie Jackson

True: a (He starred in four sports at Cheltenham High School in Pennsylvania.); d (He was tied with Ralph Kiner at 369.); e; g

False: b (He left after his sophomore year with a bonus of $85,000 from Charlie Finley, but he returned to earn a degree in biology.); c (They are not related.); f (He was MVP in 1973 with Oakland. He had 32 home runs, 117 RBIs, and he hit .293.); h (He is actually the fourth, behind Hank Aaron, Willie Mays, and Frank Robinson.)

Answer: Charlie Hough, Elias Sosa, and Burt Hooton were the Dodger pitchers. Babe Ruth hit three homers in one World Series game, twice, in the fourth games of the 1926 and 1928 World Series.

Fergie Jenkins

True: a (He broke his left hand playing in a league in the town where he was born, and that was one of the major reasons he pitched so poorly in 1975.); e (Jenkins had 2,770 strikeouts, only 49 strikeouts shy of Young's career record.); f (His 47 shutouts put him ninth on the all-time list of shutout pitchers.)

False: b (In the last five decades, that remarkable feat was also performed by the Phillies' Robin Roberts and the Braves' Warren Spahn, both of whom are in the Hall of Fame.); c (Jim Palmer and Gaylord Perry have more wins, and Steve Carlton and Tom Seaver have the same number of wins—178—as Jenkins. In other words, he is tied for third for most wins in the decade.); d (Jenkins's 247 career wins put him behind Gaylord Perry's 279 and Jim Kaat's 264.); g (That honor belongs to Gaylord Perry alone. The award went to Catfish Hunter that year. Hunter had an identical record but a slightly lower ERA. Also, Hunter's Oakland A's won their division and league.); h (His 24 wins in 1971 led the NL and his 25 wins in 1974 tied him for the AL lead.)

Answer: The Texas Rangers got Jenkins back for minor-league pitcher John Poloni and an estimated $20,000 in cash. Jenkins went on to 18–8 and 16–14 seasons.

Tommy John

True: a (After a year of inactivity, he started 39 games and recorded a 10–10 record with the Dodgers.); c (He received 35 offers, to be precise.); d; e; g; h

False: b (He has had only two 20-game seasons: 1977 with the Dodgers and 1979 with the Yankees.); f (He was second to Steve Carlton.)

Answer: The six men were Andy Messersmith, Gaylord Perry, Ferguson Jenkins, Joe McGinnity, Jesse Tannehill, and Al Orth.

Randy Jones

True: c (His 20–12 record and league-leading ERA of 2.24 placed him second in voting to Tom Seaver, who had a 22–9 record and also led the league in strikeouts. Jones was also tenth in the voting for the NL MVP.); d (In 1974, he had a record of 8–22. He was shut out in seven of those losses, given only one run in four more, and given only two runs in six more. That accounts for 17 of the 22 losses. He still managed a 4.46 ERA, a remarkable feat for a pitcher who lost 22 games.); f (By coming in first over New York Met Jerry Koosman, he joined Mike Marshall in this arcane accomplishment.); g (In 1976, he went from May 17 until June 22 without giving up a walk.); h (His record is 87–92.)

False: a (He received his degree in business from Chapman College, and he was a College All-American in baseball.); b (Claude Osteen, who pitched for 18 years in the major leagues, lives in Jones's hometown and helped him to develop his curveball and slider.); e (He got the save in the 1975 game by pitching the ninth inning and holding on to the NL lead, and he started the 1976 game and got the win.)

Answer: Bob Gibson won in 1970 with the fourth-place Cardinals, and Steve Carlton won in 1972 with the sixth-place Phillies.

Al Kaline

True: a (He was still 20 in 1955, younger by a day than Ty Cobb, the previous record holder.); b (He refused the offer to become the Tigers' first six-figure ballplayer because he didn't feel that his 1969 season justified it. He had hit .292 with 21 home runs and 69 RBIs.); c (Those five men were Ty Cobb, Stan Musial, Willie Mays, Eddie Collins, and Hank Aaron.); d (Cap Anson was 46, Honus Wagner was 44, Eddie Collins was 43, Stan Musial, Willie Mays, and Paul Waner were 42, Ty Cobb and Napoleon Lajoie were 41, and Hank Aaron and Tris Speaker were 40.); e (It was Kaline's 498th career double, off an outside fastball.); f (He played in 242 games in a row in the 1970–72 period without making an error. He went the entire 1971 season without making an error.); h (One reason is that players did not wear numbers on their uniforms back in the days of Ty Cobb.)

False: g (After waiting 16 years, he almost didn't get to play in 1968. Manager Mayo Smith moved Mickey Stanley to shortstop to make room for Kaline in the outfield. Al responded with two home runs, eight RBIs, and a .379 batting average.)

Answer: The other six are Hank Aaron, Willie Mays, Roberto Clemente, Pete Rose, Lou Brock, and Carl Yastrzemski.

Dave Kingman

True: b (He pitched four innings in two games in 1973 and gave up four earned runs on three hits and six bases on balls.); c (He led with 29 home runs and 83 RBIs.); e (He hit 37 in 1976.); f; h (He has a lifetime batting average of .241.)

False: a (He opened the season at third base in 1972 and 1974.); d (Willie Mays has held this record since 1965 with 52 home runs.); g (He led the league with 49 home runs, but he was second to Dave Winfield in RBIs.)

Answer: He hit 9 home runs with the Mets, 11 with the Padres, 4 with the Yankees, and 2 with the Angels.

Davey Lopes

True: b; c (He stole 77 and 63 bases, respectively.); d (He did it in 1975, erasing Max Carey's record of 31, set in 1922.); f (In 1974, against the Cardinals, he tied a seventy-year-old mark.)

False: a (He does not believe in weights and never touches them.); e (Both Rogers Hornsby, with 42, and Dave Johnson, with 43, hit more home runs than his 28 in 1979.); g (Jimmy Wynn also hit three home runs in one game, and in the same year—1974.); h (At the beginning of the 1980 season, his 375 put him in sixth place, behind Bert Campaneris, with 628; Joe Morgan, 601; Bobby Bonds, 441; Cesar Cedeno, 427; and Freddie Patek, 377.)

Answer: The four previous team captains were Pee Wee Reese, Duke Snider, Maury Wills, and Willie Davis.

Greg Luzinski

True: a (He spends some $20,000 a year on this.); b; c; d; e; h

False: f (He has been on the All-Star squad four times, three as a starter.); g (Although he struck out 151 times in 1975, he led the league only once, in 1977, with 140 strikeouts.)

Answer: Luzinski was runner-up to George Foster, who hit .320, with 52 home runs and 149 RBIs.

Sparky Lyle

True: d (Williams told him that he found the slider the hardest pitch to hit when he was a part-time batting instructor for the Red Sox. The conversation took place in Ocala, Florida, in 1965.); e; h

(He won two games against Los Angeles and one game against Kansas City in 1977. He also got one save in the 1976 championship against Kansas City.)

False: a (His high school did not have a baseball team, but he was a sandlot pitcher.); b (It was a steal for the Yankees who sent Mario Guerrero and Danny Cater to the Red Sox. The former was later sold to St. Louis and sent down to Tulsa. The latter had three fair seasons but played in only slightly more than 200 games.); c (He is one of the biggest pranksters in baseball today.); f (Rollie Fingers's 209 saves topped Sparky by 19.); g (He led the league with 72 games, but Bill Campbell had 31 saves to his 26.)

Answer: Mike Marshall won the Cy Young with the Dodgers in 1974. He was 15–12, saved 21, and had an ERA of 2.42.

Fred Lynn

True: a; b; e; h

False: c (From 1975 through 1979, he hit .331, .314, .260, .298, and .333.); d (He was an All-American but at the University of Southern California.); f (He's done it only twice, 105 RBIs in 1975 and 122 RBIs in 1979.); g (He did lead the league in runs in 1975 with 103, but he had only 76 in 1976.)

Answer: Carlton Fisk was the unanimous choice as Rookie of the Year in 1972, when he hit .293 with 22 home runs and 61 RBIs.

Bill Madlock

True: b (The most runs he ever scored were 85, in 1979.); f (He got four singles in the fifth game against the Orioles in 1979.); h (Madlock scored five runs in one game in 1975. Dozens of other players scored as many runs, but, in this century, only Johnny Pesky in 1946, Mel Ott in 1934 and 1944, and Frank Torre in 1957 scored six runs.)

False: a (He got some 150 offers to play college football but only 2 for baseball. He accepted the one from Keokuk, turning down an offer from the Cardinals.); c (That is what Madlock once thought, but actually Roberto Clemente did so in 1964–65 and Pete Rose did the same in 1968–69.); d (He fell below this mark only once, in 1979, when he hit a combined .298 with San Francisco and Pittsburgh.); e (Rico Carty hit .366 in 1970 and Joe Torre hit .363 in 1971.); g (He was traded for Ferguson Jenkins, not Ron Santo.)

Answer: He was hitting .190 and was terribly unhappy playing ball in the Dominican Republic, when he got the news that he had been traded to the Cubs from the Rangers. He never dreamed that he could replace Ron Santo at third and he thought that he was on his way back to the minors.

Mike Marshall

True: f (His 106 appearances with Los Angeles in 1974 are a major-league record as well as an NL one, and his 90 appearances with Minnesota in 1979 are an AL record.); g (He won both in 1974, when he appeared in 106 games and had a 15–12 record with 21 saves and a 2.42 ERA.)

False: a (He has a doctorate in education and has taught exercise physiology at Michigan State University.); b (He had almost 2,000 at-bats as a shortstop for four seasons in the minor leagues with the Phillies organization before moving to the mound.); c (He was traded for Don Bosch, a lifetime .164 hitter, who left baseball several weeks after the trade.); d (Gene Garber holds the record of 16 losses, set in 1979. Marshall shares second place with Darold Knowles and John Hiller, all with 14 losses.); e (His 685 games place him fifth behind Darold Knowles [763], Sparky Lyle [747], Jim Kaat [718], and Rollie Fingers [701].); h (His 15 wins in 1974 were two fewer than John Hiller's 17 wins, with Detroit the same year. Dale Murray also won 15, with Montreal in 1975.)

Answer: Face pitched in nine consecutive games with Pittsburgh. Marshall pitched in 13 consecutive games, winning 6 and losing 2. He had a 1.67 ERA over 24.2 innings, during which he walked only three men.

Willie McCovey

True: b (McCovey's 18 grand slams are topped only by Gehrig's 23.); d (The years were 1959 and 1977, respectively.); e (He did it in April 1973 and June 1977.); f (They did it on April 26, 1970.); h (His 520 home runs at the close of the 1979 season also put him ninth on the all-time home run list, just one behind Ted Williams.)

False: a (Thurman Munson was AL Rookie of the Year in 1970 and MVP six years later, and Fred Lynn won both awards in 1975.);

c (His 1,539 RBIs were exceeded only by Carl Yastrzemski's 1,613.); g (He is third in all categories, behind Willie Mays and Mel Ott.)

Answer: Pete Rose (3,557), Carl Yastrzemski (3,109), Rusty Staub (2,547), Tony Perez (2,399), and Rod Carew (2,394). Lou Brock, who retired after the 1979 season was over, had 3,023 hits.

Tug McGraw

True: d (It was former Yankee pitcher Ralph Terry who showed McGraw his pitch by using a golfball as a prop.); e (His 85 saves are far ahead of Lockwood's 65.); f (He holds first place, with 27 saves in 1972. He also holds second place, with 25 saves in 1973.); g (His 132 saves place him fourth, behind Fingers's 209, Lyle's 190, and Marshall's 177.)

False: a (He spent that day, in 1963, on the luggage rack of a bus traveling with a team in Lethbridge, Canada, sponsored by the Cardinals.); b (During the second half of a doubleheader against the Giants, on Easter Sunday at Shea in 1965, he struck out pinchhitter Orlando Cepeda.); c (That was Tug's brother, Hank. Tug went to Vallejo Junior College, now Solano Community College, without either scholarship or pro offers.); h (On the contrary, the eight grand slams he has allowed in his career put him dangerously close to the record of nine, held jointly by Ned Garver, Milt Pappas, Lindy McDaniel, and Jerry Reuss.)

Answer: Trading the quintessential Met was, he said, "in terms of public identity and response . . . like the Chinese trading Mao Tse-tung to the Polynesians."

Joe Morgan

True: e (He stole 470 bases in the 1970s, compared to Carew's 253.); f (He led the league in slugging with a .576 percentage in 1976.); g (He did it in 1973 and again in 1976.); h (He had 124 walks in 1973 and 132 in 1975. Incidentally, he also led in 1965, with 97.)

False: a (He had 111 RBIs in 1976.); b (Morgan won in 1975 and 1976, but Bench did not win in consecutive years.); c (Bert Campaneris stole 628 bases in his career, 27 more than Morgan.); d (Morgan has a total of 601, compared to Bonds's 440.)

Answer: In what *Baseball Digest* called one of the 20 worst trades of the 1970s, Houston got Lee May, Tommy Helms, and Jim Stewart.

Thurman Munson

True: b (His .998 fielding percentage tied the record set by Elston Howard in 1964. Dickey led the league in fielding five times and Berra and Howard led the league twice, but their fielding percentages were not higher.); c (In 1975, he played two games at first and one at third. In 1979, he also played first.); g (He hit .302 in 1970 and .318 in 1975.)

False: a (Lou Gehrig was the last Yankee captain before Munson.); d (Munson holds the World Series record by hitting nine singles in the 1976 World Series.); e (He had three 100-RBI seasons in a row: 1975 through 1977.); f (Mantle was MVP in 1962 but Elston Howard was MVP in 1963.); h (His six home runs in 1970 fell far short of the twenty-nine hit by Joe DiMaggio in 1936.)

Answer: Johnny Bench, Rookie of the Year in 1968, was MVP in 1970 and 1972. Fred Lynn, Rookie of the Year in 1975, was MVP the same year.

Bobby Murcer

True: c (He was also all-city in basketball.); d; e (In a doubleheader against Cleveland in 1970, he hit three in one game and one in the next.); f; g; h

False: a (He was traded for Paul Semall and cash.); b (Going into the 1980 season, he had 148 home runs to Nettles's 181.)

Answer: Tom Greenwade signed him for a reported $20,000 bonus.

Graig Nettles

True: a; b; c (Although he played 22 games with Minnesota that year, he still hit .297 with 84 runs, 22 home runs, and 83 RBIs with Denver.); h

False: d (He was traded with Dean Chance, Ted Uhlaender, and Bob Miller for Luis Tiant and Stan Williams.); e (He led them twice, in 1970 and 1971, with 26 and 28 home runs, respectively.); f (He has averaged over 155 games.); g (He led the league with 32 home runs in 1976, but he was runner-up to Jim Rice in 1977, with 37.)

Answer: Reggie Jackson had 922 RBIs, Yaz had 846, and Nettles was third with 831.

Phil Niekro

True: c (They were Nolan Ryan, Tom Seaver, Steve Carlton, Bert Blyleven, and Gaylord Perry.); d (They were also the most in the majors since Wilbur Wood's 48 starts with the White Sox in 1973.); e (His 2,402 strikeouts at the end of the decade put him 18th on the career strikeout list.)

False: a (Far from it; he was 28 when he became a starter in 1967.); b (Hardly. Phil led the league with 20 losses. He also led or tied the league in losses the two previous years.); f (He has a better than two-to-one ratio of strikeouts to walks: 2,402 to 1,133.); g (His 218 wins do give him the most for a right-hander, but Warren Spahn won 356. Kid Nichols had 310 wins, but that was in the last century.); h (He threw six wild pitches. He also led the NL in this category twice, in 1967 and in 1977.)

Answer: Niekro's 164 wins make him eighth, behind Palmer (186), Gaylord Perry (184), Carlton, Jenkins, and Seaver (all 178), Hunter (169), and Sutton (166).

Tony Oliva

True: a (He never had a birth certificate, so he switched the picture on his brother Tony's passport. Scouts didn't want to waste time on a "rookie" who was some five or six years older, according to the borrowed passport, than he actually was.); d (He hit .323, seven points better than runner-up Brooks Robinson.); e (In 1964, 1965, 1966, 1969, and 1970, he led the league with 217, 185, 191, 197, and 204 hits, respectively.); g (He was disabled for all but a few weeks of the 1972 season.); h (He hit .306.)

False: b (In 1961, the Twins wouldn't offer him even the lowest Class-D contract, but he went on several months later to lead their Wytheville team in the Rookie League with a .410 batting average.); c (The Giants' star, Orlando Cepeda, beat him out .368 to .365 on the last day.); f (His .325 in 1970 and his .337 in 1971 were both higher batting averages.)

Answer: Rod Carew has the most singles (1,616) and triples (90), and Harmon Killebrew has the most home runs (475).

Amos Otis

True: e (His five stolen bases against Milwaukee on September 9, 1971, were matched only by Bert Campaneris's five steals in 1976. Actually, only two players—Eddie Collins and Clyde Milan, each with six—stole more bases in one game in history.)

False: a (The Red Sox signed him in 1965, and the Mets took him in a draft in 1966. He was traded, with pitcher Bob Johnson, from the Mets to the Royals for third baseman Joe Foy.); b (He hit .301 in 1971 and .300 in 1973. He does feel bad that he missed by so little in 1978, when he hit .298.); c (On the contrary, he established a new AL record for the highest stolen-base percentage, lifetime—300 or more attempts. In 1970, he was caught only twice while stealing 33 bases, and the next year he stole 52 while getting nabbed only eight times.); d (He holds all those records. Remember that Otis averaged over 146 games a year with the Royals for the full decade, while Brett's first *full* season with the Royals was 1975.); f (Their total of 113—30 for Otis—in 1979 puts them ninth on the all-time list. Clyde Milan and Danny Moeller are first, with 137 steals in 1913.); g (Otis did win the Gold Glove three times [1971, 1973, and 1974], but so did premier second baseman Frank White [1977, 1978, and 1979].); h (Otis did this, but so did many other players, including teammates Paul Schaal, Fred Patek, and John Mayberry.)

Answer: The record was seven stolen bases in two consecutive games, and it was set by Philadelphia's Eddie Collins.

Jim Palmer

True: d (He has pitched in five All-Star games, but he has an 0–1 record.); e (His back-to-back Cy Young awards were in 1975 and 1976.); h (He was only 20 years and 11 months old when he shut out the Dodgers in the second game of the 1966 World Series.)

False: a (Although he did attend Arizona State, it was because Arizona was his home at that time. He never played baseball in college.); b (Far from it. In 1970, he tied for the league lead, with 305 innings pitched, and he had a 20–10 record with a 2.71 ERA.); c (He was signed by the Orioles as soon as he graduated from Scottsdale High School in Arizona, for a reported $60,000 bonus, and he has been with the Baltimore organization ever since.); f (Palmer's 186 wins edged out Perry by two.); g (He struck out 1,559 batters in the 1970s, placing him at number ten on the list, but a far cry from Nolan Ryan's 2,678 strikeouts.)

Answer: The other three pitchers were Mike Cuellar (20–9), Pat Dobson (20–8), and Dave McNally (21–5).

Dave Parker

True: c (George Foster of Cincinnati was MVP. He hit .320 but led the league in runs, with 124; home runs, with 52; and RBIs, with 149.); e (He was also named MVP of that game.)

False: a (Parker grew up in Cincinnati, where he starred in baseball, football, and basketball.); b (On the contrary, he was named Player of the Year in the Carolina League as he led the league in at-bats, runs [91], hits [162], doubles [30], RBIs [101], stolen bases [38], total bases [270], and putouts [250].); d (He hit .282 in 1974, but .308, .313, .338, .334, and .310 in the next five years.); f (He averaged over 18 from 1976 to 1979.); g (Bill Madlock also did it in 1975–76.); h (He did lead the league with 340 in 1978, but his 327 was second to Dave Winfield's 333 in 1979.)

Answer: The three players were Pittsburgh's Bill Madlock and Willie Stargell, and Baltimore's Kiko Garcia.

Tony Perez

True: a; b; d (He hit .309 and had 107 RBIs with San Diego.); e; f; g; h

False: c (His 954 RBIs place him second to Johnny Bench, with 1,013.)

Answer: The pitchers were Woody Fryman and Dale Murray.

Gaylord Perry

True: a; b; d (He won it with Cleveland in 1972, when he was 24–16, and he won it with San Diego in 1978, when he was 21–6.); e; g (He had 3,141 strikeouts as the 1970s ended.)

False: c (It was the first time in *AL* history.); f (Perry and Don Sutton had 50 shutouts each, but they were second to Tom Seaver, who had 52.); h (Randy Jones won it in 1976.)

Answer: The three pitchers were Bob Feller (25–16 in 1946), Dizzy Trout (27–14 in 1944), and Dizzy Dean (28–12 in 1935).

Boog Powell

True: a (He turned down the first offer so that he could play in the high school state championship. Unfortunately, he went 1 for 13.); e (Powell had 339 home runs in his career, compared to Robinson's 586.)

False: b (His father never made it beyond being a semi-pro, and it was his mother who was the avid angler.); c (In 1970, he tied the major-league record for the second year in a row, by having *no* triples. In his 16 years in the AL, he had exactly 11 triples.); d (He "owned" Chance, hitting .400 against him before Chance went to the Mets. Powell felt that Jim Kaat was the toughest pitcher he faced.); f (He was AL MVP in 1970, but most would argue that he had a much better year in 1969, when he came in second to Harmon Killebrew in MVP rating. In 1969, he hit .304 compared to .297 in 1970, hit two more home runs, and had seven more RBIs.); g (1970 was the last year he had over 100 RBIs.); h (After 16 years in the Baltimore organization, he was traded to Cleveland, who released him.)

Answer: In 1962, baseball mogul Larry MacPhail said, "Only the knife and fork will keep him from stardom."

Willie Randolph

True: e (He stole 33 bases.); f; g (He played all nine innings and made six assists.); h (He recorded 153 games, 547 at-bats, 98 runs, 13 triples, 95 walks, and 33 stolen bases; his 155 hits were second only to Rupert Jones's 166.)

False: a (He grew up in Brooklyn and went to Tilden High School.); b (He was a seventh-round choice of the Pirates in 1972.); c (He has averaged over 139 games a year.); d (Mark "The Bird" Fidrych was.)

Answer: The pitcher was Doc Medich, who had an 8–11 record with Pittsburgh and was traded to Oakland the next season.

Jim Rice

True: a; c; e; g

False: b (In 1977, he was fourth to Rod Carew, Al Cowens, and Ken Singleton, but he did win it in 1978.); d (His 149 home runs and 486 RBIs fell short of George Foster's 151 home runs and 488

RBIs.); f (Jimmie Foxx hit 50 in 1938.); h (Ted Williams and Jimmie Foxx had higher slugging percentages, .634 and .605, respectively. Fred Lynn is close behind with .526.)

Answer: The last player to have over 406 total bases in one season was Joe DiMaggio, who had 418 in 1937. The other players were Babe Ruth (457 in 1921, 417 in 1927), Lou Gehrig (447 in 1927, 419 in 1930, 410 in 1931, and 409 in 1934), and Jimmy Foxx (438 in 1932).

Brooks Robinson

True: b (He played in 2,896 games. Ty Cobb played in more games, but with two teams.); c (From 1957 through 1976 he hit .316 on 20 opening days.); d (His .971 fielding percentage is the highest.)

False: a (That restaurant belongs to John Unitas, former star quarterback for the Baltimore Colts.); e (The string was broken by Detroit's Aurelio Rodriguez in 1976.); f (He and Frank Robinson were the first two players. Boog Powell and Dave McNally have since been added.); g (He holds all these records except home runs, a category in which he is second to Boog Powell.); h (He accumulated 28 steals in his entire career. In the 1970s, he stole exactly six bases.)

Answer: In 1970, when he was the World Series MVP, he made an error on his first chance but handled the next 23, often sensationally. He stole at least two hits from the Reds' Lee May, who said that he was a human vacuum cleaner.

Frank Robinson

True: a; b (He went to Ogden, where he hit .348, with 17 home runs and 83 RBIs in only 72 games.); d (Bench has 332 home runs to Robinson's 324, and Rose has 1,657 runs and 833 extra-base hits to Robinson's 1,043 and 692.); f (He won it in 1961 with the Reds and in 1966 with the Orioles.); g (He and Henry Aaron both hit home runs in 32 ball parks in regular-season play, but Robinson added a 33rd at Three Rivers Stadium in the 1971 World Series.); h (Robinson's 583 home runs put him fourth behind Henry Aaron, Babe Ruth, and Willie Mays.)

False: c (The Reds' manager in 1956 was Birdie Tebbetts. Robinson hit .290, with 38 home runs and 83 RBIs.); e (That is what

William De Witt said, but Robinson hit 179 home runs with the Orioles and he hit over .300 in four of his six seasons there.)

Answer: The lady was Jackie Robinson's widow, and the day marked the first appearance of a black manager in the history of baseball.

Pete Rose

True: d (When he singled off Bert Blyleven in August 1979, he passed Honus Wagner's record, which was 2,426.); e (1974 was the year he hit .284); f (He had 2,045 hits in the 1970s, compared to the 1,787 of his closest rival, Rod Carew.); g (His highest RBI number was 82, in 1969.)

False: a (His father was a banker, but his uncle, Buddy Bloebaum, convinced the Reds to sign him.); b (He stole 16 bases in 1977, but the 20 he stole in 1979 are the most of his major-league career.); c (In 1979, he surpassed Cobb's accomplishment of 200 hits in nine seasons.); h (He didn't break Keeler's record; he tied it at 44 games.)

Answer: Rose's 4,678 total bases are surpassed by only 16 players, and the only active one is Carl Yastrzemski, with 4,907.

Nolan Ryan

True: a (Indeed, his record for the 1970s is barely .500: 155–146.); b; d; f (His 383 strikeouts in 1973 broke Sandy Koufax's record of 382, set in 1965.)

False: c (Sandy Koufax also pitched four no-hitters, one each in 1962, 1963, 1964, and 1965.); e (He did lead or tie the AL shutout record for three seasons, but his career record of 42 shutouts puts him far short of Johnson's 113.); g (He never led the NL in season strikeouts.); h (His 2,909 career strikeouts put him second only to Perry's 3,141.)

Answer: The remarkable feat of two no-hitters in one season has been accomplished by Johnny Vander Meer, Virgil Trucks, Allie Reynolds, and Jim Maloney.

Mike Schmidt

True: c (He led three years in a row—1974–76.); d (In those five years, he hit 180 home runs, as compared to 175 for his closest competitor, Dave Kingman.); g (He did this in 1974, 1976, 1977, and 1979.)

False: a (He played only 87 games in the minor leagues.); b (He did not play minor-league ball at all until after he graduated from Ohio University.); e (He did win the fielding awards, but he placed second in the voting, well behind Brooks Robinson.); f (He did set a new team record, but Dave Kingman hit 49 home runs that year.); h (Neither he nor Dick Allen was ever named MVP in the NL.)

Answer: Steve Carlton was named to *Sporting News* All-Star teams in 1972, 1977, and 1979.

Tom Seaver

True: a (Technically this is true, although Commissioner Eckert voided the contract because it violated the college rule.); b (He won 16 games, and the Mets won only 61 games that year, 1967.); f (He had 283 strikeouts in 1970, 289 in 1971, 251 in 1973, 243 in 1975, and 235 in 1976. He had an ERA of 2.81 in 1970, 1.76 in 1971, and 2.08 in 1973.)

False: c (He won 95 games.); d (He won the Cy Young Award three times: in 1969, 1973, and 1975.); e (He did it eight times. He struck out "only" 196 batters in 1977 and 131 in 1979.); g (He led the league in complete games once—in 1973, with 18.); h

Answer: Among all pitchers still active at the end of 1979, only Gaylord Perry and Nolan Ryan had struck out more batters in their lifetime.

Rusty Staub

True: a (Joe Adcock [1954], Willie Stargell [1970], and Steve Garvey [1977] have five extra-base hits. However, 130 other NL players also have four extra-base hits.); b (He had 11 hits, batting .423, as a Met in the 1973 Series against Oakland.); d (He hit two with Detroit and one with Texas in the AL and two with Montreal and four with New York in the NL.); e (He had five double plays in 1971, 1973, and 1974.); f (His 105 RBIs in 1975 are a team record; 8 more than Clendenon's 97 in 1970.); g (His .333 in 1967 is the highest of any Houston player.); h (He came to bat 642 times and played the entire season as a DH.)

False: c (On the contrary, Carl Yastrzemski is the only left-hander to hit into *more* double plays.)

Answer: On October 1, the Mets beat the Cubs at Wrigley Field, 6–4, and won the division title. Staub had four hits in five at-bats.

Willie Stargell

True: d (He led the league with 48 in 1971 and 44 in 1973.); f (McCovey had 520 lifetime homers, compared to Stargell's 461.); g (In 1977, he struck out 93 times but had 97 RBIs.); h (He had three home runs and four doubles.)

False: a (He won eight letters at Encinal High School in Alameda, California, participating in baseball, football, and basketball.); b (He was signed by the Pirates as a free agent when he was only 17 and assigned to D ball. He has been with the Pirates since 1958.); c (He and Reggie Jackson are tied for this record at 12 seasons.); e (Stargell is the number-one Pirate in all these categories.)

Answer: In addition to tying Keith Hernandez for the NL MVP Award, he also shared *Sports Illustrated*'s Sportsman of the Year Award with the Steelers' Terry Bradshaw.

Bruce Sutter

True: a (They drafted him on the 21st round and the Cubs signed him as a free agent the next year.); c (He won both the 1978 and 1979 games, pitching two and two-thirds innings and giving up no runs.); e (Sutter's six strikeouts in a row against the Mets was matched by Don Gullett and Andy Messersmith, but only Seaver surpassed it.); f (The other two were Nolan Ryan and Lynn McGlothen.)

False: b (He had 105 saves in four seasons.); d (John Hiller saved 38 games for Detroit in 1973.); g (He won both in 1979 when he won 6 and saved 37.); h (John Hiller's combination of 48 wins and saves was the highest.)

Answer: Clay Carroll with Cincinnati in 1972 and Rollie Fingers with San Diego in 1978 also saved 37 games.

Don Sutton

True: a (From 1966 through 1969, he set a new major-league record by losing 13 consecutive games to one club.); b (He was spectacular over 17 innings, giving up only one run while striking out 13.); c (He and Koufax's 526 strikeouts are third to Koufax's and Drysdale's 592 in 1965 and 557 in 1963.); f (He had won 217 games by the end of the decade, more than any other Dodger in history.); g; h (His 2,524 strikeouts leads Don Drysdale's 2,486 and Koufax's 2,396.)

False: d (He won the 1977 game. He has appeared in four All-Star games overall, giving up no runs in eight innings.); e (He won 166 games over that span while losing 110.)

Answer: He had 50. The record is Walter Johnson's 113 shutouts.

Luis Tiant

True: a (Luis Tiant, Sr., started with the Almendares Blues in Cuba and later, with the Cuban Stars, toured the United States. When he was 41 years old, he went 10–0 as his team won the Negro National League and defeated Monte Irvin's Newark Eagles in the playoff.); h (He struck out ten or more 32 times, compared to Sutton's 28, Drysdale's 27, Grove's 26, and Blue's 26. They are all far short of Nolan Ryan's 130 times or Sandy Koufax's 98.)

False: b (After he lost 20 in 1969, Cleveland traded him to Minnesota, which was the team that released him.); c (His 49 shutouts put him eighth on the all-time list, behind Walter Johnson, Grover Alexander, Warren Spahn, Tom Seaver, Jim Palmer, Don Sutton, and Gaylord Perry.); d (His 19 strikeouts in ten innings on July 3, 1968, against Minnesota tie him with Nolan Ryan, who struck out 19 in extra innings three times. Tom Cheney, with 21 strikeouts in 16 innings, set in 1962, still held the record at the end of the decade.); e (Their total of 547 strikeouts while with Cleveland in 1968 puts them sixth on the all-time list behind Nolan Ryan's and Bill Singer's 624 [1973], Sandy Koufax's and Don Drysdale's 592 [1965], Nolan Ryan's and Frank Tanana's 588 [1976], Koufax's and Drysdale's 557 [1963], and Rube Waddell's and Eddie Plank's 550 [1904].); f (Tiant was signed as a free agent in 1971 and went on to win 121 games from 1972 through 1978. By the way, Scott was traded to Milwaukee.); g (He won 20 in 1973 and 22 in 1974 but fell two wins short in 1975, with 18.)

Answer: Babe Ruth had nine shutouts in 1916, while winning 23 and losing 12 and posting a 1.75 ERA.

Roy White

True: b; d (He had 104 runs.); e (He played in 1,881 games, compared to Joe D's 1,736.); f (He hit .267, scored 89 runs, had 154 hits, 20 doubles, 7 triples [tied Robinson], 62 RBIs, and stole 20 bases [tied Clarke].); g (Stirnweiss stole 33 bases in 1945.); h (His total of 393 places him tenth, behind Joe Morgan, Bobby Bonds, Reggie Jackson, Cesar Cedeno, Carl Yastrzemski, Jose Cardenal, Amos Otis, Don Baylor, and Reggie Smith.)

False: a (Tresh was only 25 then and in the second year of his major-league career. In 1965, when White came up to the Yankees, he played outfield and second base behind Bobby Richardson.); c (Hal Chase [1905–13] stole 248 bases, compared to White's 233.)

Answer: White's 1,881 games put him behind Mantle's 2,401, Gehrig's 2,164, Berra's 2,116, and Ruth's 2,084.

Billy Williams

True: a (He is tenth, with 392 career home runs. Ahead of him is Henry Aaron [733], Willie Mays [660], Willie McCovey [520], Ernie Banks [512], Mel Ott [511], Eddie Mathews [503], Stan Musial [475], Willie Stargell [461], and Duke Snider [407]. Williams also had 34 home runs in the AL.); b (In 1972, Williams became the first Cub since Phil Cavarretta to lead the league in hitting.); c (He hit four doubles in one game, but over 30 other players did also.); d (He scored five runs on May 31, 1970, a feat matched by 19 players but surpassed by no one.)

False: e (He was NL Rookie of the Year in 1961 and won the batting championship in 1972.); f (He is second in each category to Ernie Banks.); g (They shared the NL lead with 205 hits.); h (He hit 30 or more home runs many times, including a career high of 42 in 1970.)

Answer: Everett Scott (1,307) played with the Red Sox and the Yankees, and Joe Sewell (1,103) played with the Indians and the Yankees. Williams had 1,117 games in a row from September 12, 1963, to September 2, 1970. This places him third on the all-time list.

Willie Wilson

True: c (He led the Gulf Coast League with 24 in 1974, the Midwest League with 76 in 1975, and the American League with 83 in

1980.); f (Of the other players who stole 50 or more bases, Le Flore hit .300 on the nose, Omar Moreno hit .282, and Billy North hit .259.)

False: a (He grew up in New Jersey and is generally regarded as the best schoolboy athlete since Olympic decathloner Milt Campbell, who won a silver at the 1952 games.); b (The offers were there, but he signed with the Royals.); d (Brock and McBride stole 148 bases between them in 1974, compared to Wilson and Otis's 113.); e (He did not become a switch-hitter until 1977.); g (On the contrary, he does not want to be known just for his speed but for his hitting.)

Answer: The category is hardest to double up, and the stat represents the number of at-bats per double plays grounded into. Willie was at bat 588 times and hit into only one double play. The next four in the league in 1979 were Mickey Rivers (106.60), Al Bumbry (94.83), Rick Cerone (93.80), and George Brett (80.63).

Carl Yastrzemski

True: c (On September 12, 1979, he got his 3,000th hit off the Yankees' Jim Beattie at Fenway.); d (He had 169 intentional walks by the end of the seventies.); e (The four were Ty Cobb, Ernie Banks, Babe Ruth, and Honus Wagner. Yaz had 102 in 1977.); f (He had 186 hits and 128 bases on balls in 1970 for a total of 314. The record is 375 and it was set in 1923 by Babe Ruth who had 205 hits and 170 bases on balls.); g (The 288 times he hit into double plays is surpassed only by Henry Aaron and Brooks Robinson, both of whom were right handers.)

False: a (The Sox signed him out of Notre Dame but he played second base and shortstop at Raleigh where he hit .377. He moved to the outfield the next season.); b (Yaz is first in all three categories. Rose is second.); h (Yaz's 404 home runs were third only to Willie McCovey's 520 and Willie Stargell's 461.)

Answer: Henry Aaron had 3,771 hits and 755 home runs; Willie Mays had 3,283 and 660; Stan Musial had 3,630 and 475. At the end of the seventies, Yaz had 3,009 hits and 404 home runs.

PITCHING

In 1920, the Baseball Rules Committee abolished the spitball and other unorthodox deliveries. They provided that each team could name two pitchers as spitball pitchers for the rest of the season, but that no spitballers would be allowed after that. In 1921, the ruling was changed to allow eight pitchers from the National League and nine from the American League to be named as spitball pitchers and to be allowed to use the spitball for the rest of their careers. One of the notable beneficiaries of the second ruling was Burleigh Grimes, then with the Brooklyn Dodgers. He went on to pitch until 1934, having his best year in 1928, when he won 25 and lost 14 with Pittsburgh.

In 1969, the Baseball Rules Committee lowered the pitcher's mound from 15 inches above the base lines and home plate to ten inches.

Both of these changes in rules are cut from the same cloth; they are intended to give the batter a better chance to hit or to make the pitcher's job even more difficult, depending on your point of view. Pitchers say that the spitball should be legalized, and hitters say that it should be outlawed.

Come multimillion-dollar contracts, exploding scoreboards, and expansion teams, come players' unions and strikes, designated hitters, and ball day, bat day, fan appreciation day, and what-have-you day, one thing in baseball never changes, and that is the one-to-one contest between pitcher and hitter. There is a never-ending debate about who is in charge in a given time period and endless discussion on how to restore the balance between the two.

Joey Jay, a pitcher who won 99 and lost 91 over a 13-year career, may find his place in history as the first graduate of Little League baseball to make the major leagues. He wrote an apologia for pitchers some 20 years ago in which he said that the reason that hitters had the upper hand was due to four factors: rules, parks, balls, and bats.

Regarding rules, the most publicized issue is that of the spitball and whether or not it should be legalized. Without going into this endless argument, let me say that spitballs remind me of strikes inasmuch as the threat of their use is often as effective as their actual use. Many a pitcher who is rumored to be a spitball pitcher has said that he is pleased to have the reputation because it gives the batter one more thing to worry about.

Regarding parks, Jay's argument was that everything—gloves, bats, methods of training—had improved except the ball parks. By improving the ball parks, he meant moving the fences back 40 or 50 feet. In his own words, "Let's give the speedy outfielders a chance to make some great plays, and let's give the poor pitchers a chance to breathe a little."

Ford Frick, onetime commissioner of baseball, predicted in 1962 that fans were eventually going to get tired of seeing a lot of home runs. A new record of 2,730 home runs had been hit in the major leagues the year before, and he was arguing not for bigger ball parks but for the legalization of the spitter. Since there were only 20 teams then and 26 teams now, and since, according to the NL Green Book and the AL Red Book, there were 3,415 home runs hit in 1979, a year that saw new attendance records set, Commissioner Frick's argument does not seem to be very convincing. Actually, since he made that statement, the average number of home runs in one season has dropped from 136 to 131 per team.

Ted Williams, brutally frank as usual, gave his own explanation for all the home runs that pitchers complain about so much. He blamed them on expansion, explaining that there are pitchers in the major leagues today who would not be there were it not for the fact that there are now 26 teams. The pitching talent is spread too thin.

The issue of whether baseballs are livelier or not comes up with boring regularity. Every few years, some magazine or another dissects the poor old horsehide, performs an autopsy on it, drops it off buildings, and submits it to a battery of tests designed for the space shuttle. The scientific findings are usually that the ball has not changed. The manufacturer usually says something like what the president of A. G. Spalding and Brothers said almost 20 years ago: "The specifications are exactly the same as they were in 1926, the year they added the cork center to the ball. We do not wind the ball any tighter, and we use the same winding, the same yarn, the same cotton, the same hides and the same hand-stitching that we've used for the last thirty-five years."

How then does one explain some of the tape-measure shots belted by Punch and Judy hitters? Maybe vitamins are to blame.

The change in the form and shape of the bat as well as the changing taste of the players regarding bats does have something to do with hitting balls harder. The thinner-handled, lighter bats of today do have more snap to them, and a lighter bat can be swung faster. Most of today's hitting stars use 31-, 32-, or 33-ounce bats, as compared to the 42-ouncer that Babe Ruth preferred. Indeed, Ruth once used a 54-ounce bat.

However good or bad today's pitchers may be, they all compete for the same honor, the Cy Young Award. Commissioner Ford Frick instituted the award in 1957, and he left it up to the Baseball Writers Association of America to choose a single pitcher as baseball's best. The Dodgers' Don Newcombe was the first winner. In 1967, Gen. William Eckert, Frick's successor, agreed with the BBWA that each league should have its own winner of the Cy Young Award.

The award for the best pitcher in either league could hardly have been named after a more appropriate player than Denton True Young. In his 22 years with five different teams, he won over 500 games. The closest record of any contemporary pitcher is Gaylord Perry's 279 wins at the end of the 1970s, followed by Jim Kaat's 264, Ferguson Jenkins's 247, and Tom Seaver's 235.

Cy Young's 2,804 strikeouts was surpassed at the end of the decade by Gaylord Perry, Bob Gibson, Nolan Ryan, Tom Seaver, Jim Bunning, and Mickey Lolich, all of whom played during the 1970s. Several other stars of the seventies, including Ferguson Jenkins, Steve Carlton, and Phil Niekro, should pass him in this department before their careers are over.

Among the Cy Young Award winners of the 1970s is three-time winner Jim Palmer, who led all pitchers with 186 wins in the decade. He was closely followed in the wins column by four other pitchers who were also Cy Young Award winners in the 1970s, namely Gaylord Perry, with 184 wins, and Steve Carlton, Ferguson Jenkins, and Tom Seaver, all tied with 178 wins.

The king of the strikeout artists in the 1970s was Nolan Ryan, with 2,678 strikeouts in the decade and 2,909 overall at the end of the 1979 season and an excellent chance of breaking Walter Johnson's all-time record of 3,508 strikeouts.

Although it is very unlikely that anyone will touch such records as Cy Young's wins or his 7,356 innings pitched, or the 41 wins in one season by Jack Chesbro, or Bob Feller's 12 one-hitters, this does not mean, by any stretch of the imagination, that today's pitchers are not just as good in their own way, particularly given the relatively recent emphasis on relief pitchers.

Consider some of the following pitching feats of the 1970s, in addition to the several noted above.

Tom Seaver struck out 19 batters in a game in 1970, striking out the last ten batters in a row. This latter is a record no one has come close to in all of baseball history.

Nolan Ryan's record of 383 strikeouts in 1973 was the highest in either league in this century, passing up Sandy Koufax's 1965 record by one strikeout.

Jim Palmer had ten shutouts in 1975, a feat surpassed by AL pitchers only four times since 1900.

Ron Guidry's .893 winning percentage (25–3) in 1978 was surpassed only by John Allen's .938 in 1973. Even so, Allen's record was only 15–1.

Until Steve Carlton struck out 310 batters in 1972 and J. R. Richard struck out 303 in 1978 and 313 in 1979, Sandy Koufax was the only other pitcher in NL history to strike out 300 or more batters in one season.

Pitching quizzes are Q and A and multiple choice.

QUIZ 1

1. Who was the only man to win the Cy Young three times in the 1970s?

2. Who were the two Yankee pitchers who won Cy Young awards in consecutive years?
3. Who had the lowest winning percentage of all Cy Young Award winners in the 1970s in the year he won?
4. Who were the two two-time Cy Young Award winners in the NL in the 1970s?
5. Who were the two pitchers with the Angels who led the AL in strikeouts eight times in a row in the 1970s?
6. The NL strikeout record was held in five seasons in the 1970s by which of the following players:
   a. Steve Carlton
   b. Gaylord Perry
   c. Tom Seaver
   d. Gary Nolan
7. Of all pitchers in both leagues, who posted the lowest ERA in the 1970s?
8. Five shutouts in one season are usually enough to make a pitcher a contender for the league lead. Only one pitcher in the 1970s had a season in which he pitched twice that amount, the most shutouts in one season in the decade. Who was he?
9. Who was the AL pitcher who led or tied for the league lead in shutouts three times in the 1970s?
10. Four AL pitchers won the Cy Young Award and led the league in ERA the same year five times. Who were the four pitchers, and which one of them did it twice?

QUIZ 2

1. Who were the two pitchers from the Padres who won Cy Young awards in the 1970s?
2. Who were the three AL pitchers named Jim who won the Cy Young Award in the 1970s?
3. Only one AL pitcher won the Cy Young Award in the 1970s with fewer than 20 wins. Who was he?
4. Who was the NL pitcher who won the Cy Young Award in the 1970s with only a .500 percentage and fewer than ten wins?
5. Who were the other two NL pitchers who won Cy Young awards in years in which they did not have 20 or more wins?
6. Who were the two NL pitchers, once teammates, who led or tied for the league lead in shutouts twice each, in the 1970s?
7. Who was the only AL pitcher to lead the league in winning

percentage, ERA, and shutouts and who also won the Cy Young Award, all in the same year?

8. In 1973, Nolan Ryan set the all-time, single-season strikeout record. The number of batters he struck out was:
   a. 323
   b. 343
   c. 363
   d. 383
9. Oakland had three different pitchers lead in the AL in ERA in the 1970s. Can you name them?
10. The pitcher who had the lowest ERA in the NL in 1970 posted a 2.81, which was the highest number in both leagues for an ERA winner in the decade. Who was the pitcher?

QUIZ 3

1. Who were the two brothers who won Cy Young awards in the 1970s?
2. Who was the pitcher who had more wins in one season than any Cy Young Award winner in the 1970s?
3. Who were the two NL pitchers who led the league in ERA and won the Cy Young Award in the same years?
4. Who were the only two unanimous selections for the Cy Young Award in the 1970s?
5. Who struck out more batters in one season in the 1970s than any other NL pitcher?
6. Who were the two pitchers who led the league in ERA twice in the 1970s?
7. Two NL pitchers held the strikeout record twice in the 1970s. Which one of the following combinations were they?
   a. Steve Carlton and Gaylord Perry
   b. Steve Carlton and J. R. Richard
   c. J. R. Richard and Bob Gibson
   d. Bob Gibson and Ferguson Jenkins
8. Who was the only man to win Cy Young awards in both leagues in the 1970s?

QUIZ 4

1. Thirty no-hitters were thrown by 26 pitchers in the 1970s. Who were the two pitchers who had six no-hitters between them?
2. Who were the two brothers who had no-hitters in the 1970s?

3. Who were the two pitchers who threw no-hitters in the 1970s who had previously thrown no-hitters?
4. The names of three of the starting pitchers in the four no-hitters of 1976 were John. How many can you name?
5. When one pitcher threw two no-hitters in 1973, he matched a feat last accomplished in 1952. Who was that Detroit Tiger who pitched two no-hitters in 1952?
6. Who was the "other" Angel pitcher who had a no-hitter in the 1970s?
7. The Pittsburgh Pirates had two pitchers who threw no-hitters in the 1970s. Can you name them?
8. The no-hitter of July 28, 1976, in which the Chicago White Sox beat the Oakland A's was unique in two ways. The first involved the pitchers and the second was the score. What were these unique features?
9. Which of these teams did *not* have a no-hitter in the 1970s?
   a. Pittsburgh Pirates
   b. Boston Red Sox
   c. Chicago Cubs
   d. Cleveland Indians
10. In 1971 and 1973, the Chicago Cubs won three no-hitters with three different pitchers. How many can you name?

Quiz 1—Answers

1. Jim Palmer won it in 1973, 1975, and 1976.
2. Sparky Lyle won it in 1977, and Ron Guidry won it in 1978.
3. Gaylord Perry's 24–16 record with Cleveland in 1972 was the lowest and worst of the decade: .600.
4. Steve Carlton won the Cy Young Award in 1972 and 1977, and Tom Seaver won it in 1973 and 1975.
5. Nolan Ryan led the AL in strikeouts from 1972 through 1979, interrupted once by his teammate Frank Tanana, who won it in 1975.
6. c. Tom Seaver led the NL in strikeouts in 1970, 1971, 1973, 1975, and 1976.
7. Ron Guidry's 1.74 ERA in 1978 was the lowest of the decade. He gave up only 61 runs in 274 innings.
8. Baltimore's Jim Palmer had ten shutouts in 1975. Nolan Ryan, Bert Blyleven, Ron Guidry, and Don Sutton followed closely with nine shutouts in one year.
9. Nolan Ryan led the league with nine in 1972 and seven in 1976.

He had five shutouts in 1979, to tie Mike Flanagan and Dennis Leonard.

10. The four pitchers were Vida Blue, Jim Palmer, Catfish Hunter, and Ron Guidry. Palmer is the man who performed this dual feat twice.

Quiz 2—Answers

1. Randy Jones won it in 1976, and Gaylord Perry won it in 1978.
2. Everyone guesses Jim Perry and Jim Palmer, but many forget that Jim is also the first name of Catfish Hunter.
3. Sparky Lyle had a 13–5 record in 1977. However, in that year, he also had 26 saves, appeared in 72 games, and had a 2.17 ERA.
4. Bruce Sutter had a 6–6 record in 1979, but he also led the NL in saves that year, with 37.
5. The other two NL pitchers were Tom Seaver, who had a 19–10 record in 1973, and Mike Marshall, who had a 15–12 record in 1974.
6. Jon Matlack led the league with seven shutouts in 1974, and he tied John Montefusco with six shutouts in 1976. Tom Seaver led the league with seven shutouts in 1977, and he tied Joe Niekro and Steve Rogers with five shutouts in 1979.
7. Ron Guidry did it all in 1978. He struck out 260, and had a 1.74 ERA, an .893 winning percentage (25–3), and nine shutouts.
8. d. Ryan's 383 strikeouts broke Sandy Koufax's record of 382, set with the L.A. Dodgers in 1965.
9. Most people get Vida Blue (1.82 in 1971) and Catfish Hunter (2.49 in 1974), but a lot of people forget Diego Segui's 2.56 in 1970.
10. It was Tom Seaver. He won again the next year with a 1.76, the second-lowest number of the decade.

Quiz 3—Answers

1. Jim and Gaylord Perry.
2. Steve Carlton was 27–10 in 1972.
3. Steve Carlton in 1972 and Tom Seaver in 1973.
4. Steve Carlton in 1972 and Ron Guidry in 1978 were unanimous selections.

5. J. R. Richard struck out 313 batters in 1979.
6. Jim Palmer led the league in ERA in 1973 and 1975, and Ron Guidry did in 1978 and 1979.
7. b. Steve Carlton struck out 310 in 1972 and 240 in 1974, while J. R. Richard struck out 303 in 1978 and 313 in 1979.
8. Gaylord Perry won with Cleveland in 1972 and with San Diego in 1978.

Quiz 4—Answers

1. Everyone remembers Nolan Ryan's four no-hitters, but many tend to forget Steve Busby's two, in 1973 against Detroit and in 1974 against Milwaukee.
2. Bob Forsch, with St. Louis, threw a no-hitter against Philadelphia in 1978, and brother Ken, with Houston, threw one against Atlanta in 1979.
3. Ken Holtzman and Bill Stoneman also pitched no-hitters in 1969, as well as in the 1970s.
4. The three Johns were Candelaria, Montefusco, and Odom, also known as "Blue Moon."
5. Virgil "Fire" Trucks pitched one no-hitter against Washington in May and another against the Yankees in August.
6. Clyde Wright was the first Angel to pitch a no-hitter on July 3, 1970.
7. Dock Ellis pitched the first no-hitter of the decade on June 12, 1970, against San Diego. John Candelaria pitched his no-hitter on August 9, 1976, against the Dodgers.
8. The first unique feature was that the pitchers, John Odom and Francisco Barrios, teamed up for the win, an event which had not occurred since 1967. The second unique feature was that the losing team scored a run, and that had not happened since 1968.
9. b. The Boston Red Sox did not have a no-hitter in the 1970s. Pittsburgh had the no-hitters by Dock Ellis and John Candelaria; the Cubs had three: Ken Holtzman's, Burt Hooton's, and Milt Pappas's; the Indians had those by Dick Bosman and Denis Eckersley.
10. The three Cubs pitchers were Ken Holtzman, Burt Hooton, and Milt Pappas.

HITTING

In 1957, when the late Gil Hodges was starting his fifth year as manager of the Washington Senators, he wrote an article titled ".300 Hitters Are Doomed." He discussed what he perceived as the hitting crisis that had overtaken baseball, and he gave the opinions of such experts as Stan Musial, Ted Williams, Ralph Kiner, Sandy Koufax, Don Drysdale, and the ageless Gaylord Perry. Some of the reasons most often given for this "hitting crisis" were: better gloves, better fielders, night games, and the increased frequency with which relief pitchers were used.

The unanimous culprit for poor hitting, however, was the slider. "It has revolutionized baseball and knocked down batting averages," said Musial, who went on to predict that we would never see high batting averages again.

Stan the Man, who had a lifetime batting average of .331, called the slider an invention of the devil, an optical illusion. He distinguished it from the curve by pointing out that it didn't break big. "It comes up like a fastball and then swerves in just a few inches so that you never hit it with good wood," he said.

On the Johnny Carson show one night, Ted Williams, baseball's last .400 hitter, said that the hardest single thing to do in any sport was to hit a major-league curveball. Whether slider or curve, or for that matter whether fastball or knuckleball, the problem is the same, and that is how to get good wood on the ball.

Leonard Koppett, a scholar of the game and one of its most interesting writers, wrote a brilliant article on this problem several years ago, and I will paraphrase the problem of hitting as he so cogently presented it.

The ball is a sphere of less than three inches in diameter which is often thrown at speeds of over 90 miles an hour, and the bat is a cylinder, a tapered cylinder, with a diameter of not more than 2.75 inches at its widest point. When they meet, the actual area of impact, given the flattening of both objects, is about a quarter of an inch wide. The ball is moving in an arc and so is the bat, but of course they are moving in opposite directions. The angle at which they make impact is what determines the trajectory of the hit ball. If the middle of the thickness of the bat hits below the middle of the ball, it will go up; if the middle of the thickness of the bat hits above the middle of the ball, it will go down; and so on.

Also consider that a ball going 90 miles per hour translates into a speed of 132 feet per second. Since the distance from the front of the plate to the point at which the pitcher releases the ball is well under 60 feet, that means that the batter has between two-fifths and three-fifths of a second in which to pick up the ball as it leaves the pitcher's hand, plot the trajectory, and start the bat moving in the proper arc and with the proper force.

To the factors above must be added three additional considerations. First, the ball does not follow a straight path, so the batter must keep making additional in-flight adjustments, to use Koppett's space-travel vocabulary. Second, the batter must or should stop his swing if he estimates that the ball is out of the strike zone. Third, the batter must constantly look for the brush-back pitch, and he must be prepared to bail out if the sphere of approximately five ounces is headed toward his body. Thrown at major-league speeds, the baseball can cause injury or, at least, great pain if it hits the body, and it can often put the batter out of the lineup for several days. If it hits a certain part of the head, protective batting helmet notwithstanding, the baseball can be lethal. That is how Mr. Koppett described the problem of hitting.

It all sounds very complicated, but hitting major-league pitching is complicated. Ted Williams took all these factors into account plus a good deal more before he swung at a pitch. If you or I did the same, we would never have taken the bats off our shoulder when our moms or dads threw up that first underhanded pitch with the accompanying encouragement of "Swing the bat. Hit the ball."

Swinging the bat and hitting the ball are all there really is to hitting, but, as we have seen, it is not as easy as it sounds. To hit major-league pitching with consistency requires a combination of physical attributes and knowledge that few of us possess or are willing to spend years developing.

Most players in the minor leagues do have all the physical tools needed for the big leagues, but few are willing to pay the price to gather all the knowledge and information it takes to become a major-league hitter.

Roy Sievers, a 1957 batting champion, reported in *Sports Illustrated* almost 25 years ago that Ted Williams once asked him if he watched the pitchers all the time. "No, not all the time" replied Sievers. Williams said, "You should. You should watch them every minute, watch their motion, over and over again, watch what they throw to you, what they throw to you at certain times, what they throw to other hitters. Watch how they throw the fastball, where it goes, and how they throw the curve. Watch them *all* the time."

It is said that Williams could tell the spin of the ball four or five feet after it left the pitcher's hand; Musial said that he could see the pitch seven or eight feet away from the pitcher and *know* whether it was going to be a good pitch or not, depending on who the pitcher was. Watching seems to pay off when it comes to hitting.

When thinking about hitting, one must also keep in mind the factor of consistency. A lot of people can take a couple of cuts in a batting cage and hit a 90-mile-per-hour pitch. But a regular player in the major leagues has 500 or 600 official at-bats in a season. Pete Rose, for example, led the majors with 6,523 at-bats during the 1970s, that is, an average of 652.3 at-bats per season. For every 100 at-bats, he recorded 31.4 hits. He got over 200 hits a season six times during the 1970s, breaking Ty Cobb's record of nine seasons with over 200 hits. Rose *averaged* 204.5 hits a season during the 1970s. That is what hitting with consistency means.

Sages throughout history have cast doubt on future generations, and the pessimism of Gil Hodges and others about hitters not yet born proved to be no more true than that of all the naysayers before them. The average batting averages of the hitter leading the National League and the American League throughout the 1950s were .345 and .347, respectively. In the 1960s, those averages dipped to .340 and .325, but they rose again in the 1970s to .346 and .344.

Exciting new hitting stars emerged with the decade of the 1970s, and they will take their places high in the record books with the greatest hitters of all time. As the decade ended, Henry Aaron had surpassed the "unbeatable" home run record of Babe Ruth by a full 41 home runs. Willie Mays, Frank Robinson, Harmon Killebrew, Willie McCovey, and Ernie Banks, all of whom played during the 1970s, were among the select group of 12 hitters who had over 500 career home runs.

In the 1970s, Lou Brock, Al Kaline, and Roberto Clemente joined the very exclusive 3,000-hit club, as did Pete Rose and Carl Yastrzemski, both still very active at the end of the decade.

At the close of the 1979 season, Carl Yastrzemski had 1,613 RBIs, placing him fourteenth on the all-time list of RBI producers, well ahead of such vaunted hitters as Napoleon Lajoie, Rogers Hornsby, Tris Speaker, Joe DiMaggio, and Mickey Mantle.

Perhaps it is true that baseball will never again see such a pure hitter and as dedicated a student of hitting as Ted Williams. At the same time, however, it must be admitted that Rod Carew will give him a run for his money. Carew had a .333 lifetime batting average at the end of the decade and .343 for the 1970s, as compared to Williams's .344 career average. He led the AL in hitting seven times, six times in the 1970s, as compared to the six times Williams led the league. Carew's .388 in 1977 falls short of Williams's .406 in 1941, but it was the best in 20 years, since Williams also hit .388 in 1957.

Hitting is still another area where it can be shown that baseball is better than ever.

Hitting quizzes are Q and A, true/false, and multiple choice.

QUIZ 1

1. Which of these players did not win consecutive batting championships in the 1970s?
   a. Dave Parker c. Bill Madlock
   b. George Brett d. Rod Carew
2. In the 1970s, who led the NL with the most singles in any one season?
   a. Pete Rose c. Joe Torre
   b. Dave Parker d. Mike Schmidt
3. Which one of these players did not lead his league in triples at least twice in the 1970s?

a. Gary Templeton
b. Joe Morgan
c. Mickey Rivers
d. Rod Carew

4. Which one of these players led his league in total bases three years in a row?
   a. Greg Luzinski
   b. Jim Rice
   c. Dave Parker
   d. Billy Williams
5. Who won the AL batting championship with the lowest batting average of the decade?
   a. Tony Oliva
   b. Rod Carew
   c. George Brett
   d. Fred Lynn
6. Which one of these NL teams had three players who each led the league in singles at least once in the 1970s?
   a. Cincinnati
   b. Philadelphia
   c. St. Louis
   d. Pittsburgh
7. Who were the three players?
8. Pete Rose led the NL in doubles four times in the 1970s. How many of the leaders for the other six years can you name?
9. True or false: Pete Rose led the NL in doubles four times in the 1970s.

QUIZ 2

1. Which of these pairs of players led their leagues with the highest batting averages in any one year in the 1970s—.366 in the NL and .388 in the AL?
   a. Rico Carty and Tony Oliva
   b. Dave Parker and Rod Carew
   c. Keith Hernandez and Alex Johnson
   d. Rico Carty and Rod Carew
2. In the 1970s, who led the AL with the most singles in any one season?
   a. Chet Lemon
   b. Rod Carew
   c. Cesar Tovar
   d. George Brett
3. Which one of these players did not lead his league in triples at least twice in the 1970s?
   a. Ralph Garr
   b. George Brett
   c. Jim Rice
   d. Rod Carew
4. In the NL, Henry Aaron had the highest slugging average of the 1970s, with a .699 average in 1971. The next highest was .646 in

1973. Which of the following Pirates had the NL's second-highest slugging average of the decade?
   a. Dave Parker c. Willie Stargell
   b. Matty Alou d. George Foster
5. Which of these players did not set his club's season record for singles in the 1970s?
   a. Tito Fuentes c. Felix Millan
   b. Lou Brock d. Ralph Garr
6. Which of these NL teams had two players who each led the league in doubles in the 1970s?
   a. Pittsburgh c. Philadelphia
   b. Cincinnati d. Los Angeles
7. Who were the two players?
8. Who was the designated hitter from Kansas City who led the AL in doubles in 1977?
9. True or false: When Pete Rose's 51 doubles led the league in 1978, that was the lowest number to lead the league in over 15 years.

QUIZ 3

1. In the 1970s, who are the two players who tied for the NL lead for the most hits in any one season?
   a. Pete Rose c. Steve Garvey
   b. Joe Torre d. Ralph Garr
2. Three players tied for the AL lead in doubles in 1970, and two of them were teammates. Which of these trios were they?
   a. Hal McRae, Lou Piniella, George Scott
   b. Thurman Munson, Roy White, Rod Carew
   c. Tony Oliva, Cesar Tovar, Amos Otis
   d. Fred Lynn, Carl Yastrzemski, Willie Wilson
3. Which one of these players did not lead his league in home runs in consecutive years?
   a. Johnny Bench c. Jim Rice
   b. Mike Schmidt d. George Foster
4. Which of these players posted the highest slugging percentage in one year in the 1970s in the AL?
   a. Dick Allen c. Jim Rice
   b. Fred Lynn d. Reggie Jackson

5. Only one player had over 1,000 RBIs during the 1970s. Which one of the following players was it?
   a. Rod Carew
   b. Johnny Bench
   c. Reggie Jackson
   d. Rusty Staub
6. Which one of these AL teams had two players who led the league in home runs three times in the 1970s?
   a. Oakland
   b. Chicago
   c. Boston
   d. Kansas City
7. Who were the two players?
8. One player led the AL in one year in the 1970s in the following categories: most hits, most triples, most home runs, most total bases, and highest slugging percentage. Who had that great year in 1978?
9. True or false: In 1979, Pete Rose moved up to third on the all-time list of doubles hitters.

QUIZ 4

1. In the 1970s, who led the AL with the most hits in any one season?
   a. Jim Rice
   b. George Brett
   c. Rod Carew
   d. Fred Lynn
2. Two players from Kansas City tied or led the AL in triples in the 1970s a total of three times. Which of these pairs are they?
   a. Amos Otis and George Brett
   b. George Brett and Fred Patek
   c. Hal McRae and Lou Piniella
   d. Lou Piniella and Amos Otis
3. Only one player hit over 50 home runs in one year in the 1970s. Which one of the following sluggers was it?
   a. Jim Rice
   b. Willie Stargell
   c. Frank Howard
   d. George Foster
4. Who won the NL batting championship with the lowest batting average of the decade?
   a. Rico Carty
   b. Billy Williams
   c. Pete Rose
   d. Keith Hernandez
5. No player had 300 home runs during the 1970s, but one did have 296. Which one of these players was it?
   a. Johnny Bench
   b. Reggie Jackson
   c. Willie Stargell
   d. Bobby Bonds

6. Which one of these AL teams had three players who led the league in slugging percentage five times in the 1970s?
   a. Milwaukee
   b. Minnesota
   c. Boston
   d. Oakland
7. Who were the three players?
8. Who led the AL in most hits and most doubles in 1970s and won the batting championship in 1971?
9. True or false: When Pete Rose hit 181 singles in 1973, that was the highest number of singles ever hit in one season in the NL.

Quiz 1—Answers

1. b. Parker won in 1977 and 1978; Madlock won in 1975 and 1976; Carew won in 1972 through 1975, and 1977 and 1978.
2. a. Pete Rose had 181 singles in 1973.
3. b. Morgan led just once, in 1971.
4. b. Jim Rice led the AL in total bases in 1977, 1978, and 1979 with 382, 406, and 360 total bases, respectively.
5. b. Rod Carew's .318 in 1972 was the lowest average of the AL batting champions of the decade.
6. b
7. Dave Cash in 1974 and 1975, Larry Bowa in 1978, and Pete Rose in 1979.
8. Wes Parker (1970), Cesar Cedeno (1971), Cedeno and Willie Montanez (tied in 1972), Willie Stargell (1973), Dave Parker (1977), and Keith Hernandez (1979).
9. True. He led the NL in 1974 through 1976 and again in 1978.

Quiz 2—Answers

1. d
2. b. Rod Carew had 180 singles in 1974.
3. c. Rice led just once, in 1971.
4. c
5. b. Brock's 156 singles in 1972 did not set a season record for the Cardinals. It was set by Jesse Burkett, with 180 in 1901.
6. a
7. Willie Stargell in 1973 and Dave Parker in 1977.
8. Hal McRae led the league with 54 doubles, the highest number of the decade. He also hit 41 of them as a DH.

9. False. It was the highest number since Frank Robinson hit 51 doubles with Cincinnati in 1962.

Quiz 3—Answers

1. a and b. Torre had 230 hits in 1971, and Rose had 230 hits in 1973.
2. c. They had 36 doubles each.
3. a. Bench led the NL in home runs twice, in 1970 and 1972, but not in consecutive years.
4. c. Jim Rice's .637 slugging percentage was the highest of the decade in the AL.
5. b. Bench had 1,013 RBIs in the decade.
6. b
7. Bill Melton had 33 home runs in 1971, and Dick Allen had 37 in 1972 and 32 in 1974.
8. Jim Rice.
9. True. His total of 612 at the end of the decade placed him just behind Stan Musial and Honus Wagner.

Quiz 4—Answers

1. c. Rod Carew had 239 hits in 1977.
2. b. Patek had 11 triples in 1971, and Brett had 13 in 1975 and 14 in 1976.
3. d. George Foster hit 52 home runs in 1977.
4. b. Billy Williams's .333 in 1972 was the lowest average of the NL batting champions of the decade.
5. c. Jackson was a close second with 292 home runs, and Bench was a close third with 290.
6. c
7. Carl Yastrzemski in 1970, Fred Lynn in 1975 and 1979, and Jim Rice in 1977 and 1978.
8. Tony Oliva
9. False. Lloyd Waner is first with 198 singles; Matty Alou's 183 is second; Rose's 181 tied him for third with Lefty O'Doul, Richie Ashburn, and Lloyd Waner.

BASES ON BALLS

One statement that has surely been heard or uttered by every baseball fan, player, announcer, manager, and coach who ever lived is "Oh, those bases on balls! They'll kill you every time." Not only does it seem as though the winning run is too often caused by a walk, but, in reality, the free ticket to first base does change the pace and substance of the game, both offensively and defensively.

The base on balls unnerves the pitcher and hurts his concentration. Throwing too many pitches to a batter, getting behind him in the count, and ultimately walking him also changes the play of the infielders. As they wait and wait for the ball to be hit, they begin to lose their fine edge, and, slowly but surely, they begin to straighten up, come off their toes, and settle back on their heels. Too often the result is that a sharply hit grounder that should have been a double-play ball becomes a hit through the infield.

On the other hand, a walk is a big shot in the arm for the team at bat, particularly if it is delivered to a lead-off batter. Some combination of a steal and a hit or a hit, an error, and a sacrifice fly, puts the offensive team on the scoreboard. As Paul Splittorff explained to sportswriter Del Black, most pitchers average a hit for about every inning pitched. This means that a walk gets the pitcher in real trouble because that puts two men on base and anything can happen. One of the things that could happen is another base on balls, a sure signal to the manager and pitching coach that the pitcher has lost his control. While the relief pitcher is warming up, the man on the mound aims one down the pipe and some lucky batter fattens up his RBI total.

The greatest batter in history in drawing passes to first base, both in one season and in a career, is none other than the great Bambino. While Babe Ruth was amassing one hitting record after another, he was also piling up a career total of 2,056 bases on balls.

Although it is true that this record of Ruth's seems safe for many years to come, it is also true that five players who were still active at the end of the 1970s are on the list of the top 30 in lifetime walks. And several others who ended their careers during the 1970s are also on that list.

Ted Williams could have broken Babe's record if he had not been possessed by that pride that made him so great. He was only 38 walks behind Ruth's record, and, with his eye, he should have been able to get that many in less than one season, had he wished to play at what he considered less than his prime condition.

Early Wynn and Bob Feller, two of the greatest pitchers in the history of the Cleveland Indians and baseball itself, rank numbers one and two in giving up bases on balls. Right up there on the list of the top thirty pitchers in giving up walks are many other greats such as Red Ruffing, Warren Spahn, Walter Johnson, Allie Reynolds, Bob Lemon, and Cy Young himself. It should come as no surprise that so many great pitchers are on this list of dubious achievement, because great pitchers tend to have more starts, pitch more innings, and play for more years. Although it took Wynn 23 years to get to the top of the list, he stands a very good chance of being replaced during the 1980 season by a young man who will be in his 14th year in the majors. By the time you read this, you will know.

Two other active pitchers are also on this top-30 list, and they are very likely to move up rapidly in the standings before their careers are over.

So, fans of today, test yourselves on the Kings of the Walk of the 1970s, both those who give and those who receive.

Bases on Balls quizzes are Q and A, true/false, and multiple choice.

QUIZ 1

1. Which one of the following pitchers is among the all-time top-ten leaders in walks?
   a. Woody Fryman
   b. Nolan Ryan
   c. Luis Tiant
   d. Juan Marichal

2. Which one of the following pitchers has given up the most bases on balls in his career?
   a. Gaylord Perry c. Bob Gibson
   b. Vida Blue d. Steve Carlton
3. Which one of the following pitchers does *not* hold a team's season record for most bases on balls?
   a. Jerry Koosman c. J. R. Richard
   b. Phil Niekro d. Nolan Ryan
4. If you liked that one, try again. Which one of *these* pitchers does *not* hold a team's season record for most bases on balls?
   a. Jim Palmer c. Jim Bibby
   b. Bill Stoneman d. Tom Underwood
5. Which of the following pitchers walked the fewest number of batters in 1979?
   a. Tom Seaver c. Ron Guidry
   b. Tommy John d. Mike Flanagan
6. Which of them walked the fewest number of batters in 1977?
7. Each of the pitchers listed below was among the top three pitchers in the AL in at least one season in the 1970s. Which one gave up the fewest walks per nine innings in 1970, 1971, and 1972?
   a. Jim Kaat c. Fritz Peterson
   b. Bert Blyleven d. Ken Holtzman
8. Each of the pitchers listed below was among the top three pitchers in the NL in at least one season in the 1970s. Which one gave up the fewest walks per nine innings in 1970 and 1971?
   a. Juan Marichal c. Claude Osteen
   b. Phil Niekro d. Ferguson Jenkins
9. Which of the following pitchers had the lowest average walks per nine innings in 1979?
   a. Mike Caldwell c. Ron Guidry
   b. Scott McGregor d. Lynn McGlothen
10. Answer the following statements true or false.
    a. Nolan Ryan has walked more batters than Bob Feller did.
    b. Steve Carlton has walked more batters than Cy Young did.
    c. Nolan Ryan led the AL in walks six times in the 1970s.
    d. Phil Niekro, Vida Blue, Nolan Ryan, and Craig Swan each gave up more than 100 bases on balls in 1979.

QUIZ 2

1. Which one of the following batters is among the all-time top-ten leaders in walks?
   a. Willie McCovey
   b. Pete Rose
   c. Carl Yastrzemski
   d. Reggie Jackson
2. Which one of the following batters has gotten the most walks in his career?
   a. Henry Aaron
   b. Gene Tenace
   c. Joe Morgan
   d. Pete Rose
3. Which one of the following batters does *not* hold a team's season record for most bases on balls?
   a. Gorman Thomas
   b. Reggie Jackson
   c. Rupert Jones
   d. Gene Tenace
4. If you liked that one, try a slightly different version of that question. Which *two* batters hold *two different teams'* season records for most bases on balls?
   a. John Mayberry
   b. Ken Singleton
   c. Mickey Rivers
   d. Rod Carew
5. Who led the majors in walks in 1979?
   a. Jim Rice
   b. Darrell Porter
   c. Willie Randolph
   d. George Brett
6. Which of these batters drew the most walks in 1979?
   a. Andre Thornton
   b. Fred Lynn
   c. Ron Le Flore
   d. Mike Schmidt
7. Each of the batters listed below was among the top three in walks in at least one season in the 1970s. Which one led the NL in 1972 and 1975, was third in 1973, and second in 1974?
   a. Johnny Bench
   b. Jim Wynn
   c. Joe Morgan
   d. Rusty Staub
8. Each of the batters listed below was among the top three in walks in at least one season in the 1970s. Which one led the AL in 1971, was second in 1970, and was third in 1972?
   a. Harmon Killebrew
   b. Frank Howard
   c. Roy White
   d. Carl Yastrzemski
9. Which one of the following players had *more than* 50 walks and struck out *fewer than* 50 times in 1979?
   a. Chet Lemon
   b. Cecil Cooper
   c. Al Oliver
   d. George Brett

10. Answer the following statements true or false.
    a. Reggie Jackson led the AL in intentional walks in 1979.
    b. Joe Morgan averaged more than 110 walks per season during the 1970s.
    c. Joe Morgan holds the NL record of 148 bases on balls in one season.
    d. Henry Aaron may have broken the Babe's home-run record, but he missed his lifetime walk record by well over 600.

Quiz 1—Answers

1. b. Ryan is fourth on the all-time list, with 1,646 walks going into the 1980 season.
2. c. Gibson gave up 1,336 walks, as compared to Carlton's 1,202, Perry's 1,188, and Blue's 798.
3. a. Koosman does not hold any team's record for most bases on balls in one season. Phil Niekro holds the Braves' record (164 in 1977); Richard holds the Astros' record (151 in 1976); the ubiquitous Nolan Ryan holds the record for both the Mets (116 in 1971) and the Angels (204 in 1977).
4. a. Jim Palmer does not hold any team's record for most bases on balls in one season; Bob Turley set Baltimore's record of 181 back in 1954. Stoneman holds the Expos' record (146 in 1971); Bibby holds the Rangers' record (116 in 1974); Underwood holds the record for the Blue Jays (140 in 1978).
5. a. Tom Seaver walked 61, as compared to John's 65, Guidry's 71, and Flanagan's 70.
6. b. Tommy John walked only 50 in 1977, as compared to Seaver's 66, Guidry's 65, and Flanagan's 70.
7. c. Peterson gave up 1.38, 1.38, and 1.58 walks per nine innings in those three years.
8. d. Jenkins gave up 1.73 and an amazing 1.02 walks per nine innings in those two years.
9. b. Scott McGregor led both leagues with 1.18 walks per nine-inning game. Caldwell had 1.49, Guidry had 2.71, and McGlothen had 2.33.
10. a. False. Feller walked 1,764 to Ryan's 1,646.
    b. False. Young walked 1,209 to Carlton's 1,202.
    c. True. He not only led the AL in walks in 1972, 1973, 1974,

1976, 1977, and 1978, but he was second to Mike Torrez in 1975 and 1979.

d. False. Niekro walked 107, Blue walked 111, Ryan walked 114, but Swan walked only 57.

Quiz 2—Answers

1. c. Yaz's 1,639 bases on balls puts him fifth behind Babe Ruth, Ted Williams, Mickey Mantle, and Mel Ott.
2. c. Joe Morgan has 1,466 walks, as compared to Aaron's 1,402, Tenace's 1,281, and Rose's 1,180.
3. b. Gorman Thomas holds the Brewers' record (98 in 1979); Rupert Jones holds the Mariners' record (85 in 1979); Gene Tenace holds the Padres' record (125 in 1977). Reggie will not come close to the Yankee record of 170 walks, set by Babe Ruth in 1923, and Sal Bando holds the record for the A's, with 118 in 1970.
4. a and b. Mayberry holds the season records for both the Royals (122 in 1973) and the Blue Jays (69 in 1979), and Singleton holds the season records for both the Orioles (118 in 1975) and the Expos (123 in 1973).
5. b. Porter drew 121 walks, as compared to Rice's 57, Randolph's 95, and Brett's 51.
6. d. Mike Schmidt got 120 bases on balls, as compared to Thornton's 90, Lynn's 82, and Le Flore's 52.
7. c. Morgan was first in 1972 and 1975 with 115 and 132 walks. He was third to Evans and Singleton in 1973, and he was second to Evans in 1974.
8. a. Killebrew had 114 walks in 1971, was second to Frank Howard in 1970, and was third to Dick Allen and Roy White in 1972.
9. d. George Brett walked 51 times and struck out only 36 times in 1979. As a matter of fact, Brett was the hardest man to strike out in the AL.
10. a. False. Ken Singleton led the AL with 16 intentional walks.
    b. True. He walked 1,181 times in those ten years.
    c. False. The NL record is 148 bases on balls in one season, but it is held jointly by Eddie Stanky (1945 with the Dodgers) and Jim Wynn (1969 with the Astros).
    d. True. He fell short by 654 bases and, interestingly, he played one year more than Ruth.

MOST VALUABLE PLAYER

The Most Valuable Player Award, as it exists today, was instituted in 1931, and Frank Frisch and Lefty Grove were the winners that year. The award has been surrounded by controversy since that time, and hardly a year goes by that the fans do not find good cause to start another heated argument about its various inequities.

One source of controversy is what George Vass, in *Baseball Digest,* calls the "pitcher-versus-hitter dilemma." One school of thought holds that the MVP is the domain of hitters, almost exclusively. The logic is that the award should go to a player making the greatest contribution on a day-to-day basis, and pitchers obviously do not play every day.

A relatively small number of pitchers have won the MVP over the years, including Bobby Schantz, Jim Konstanty, Sandy Koufax, and Denny McLain, to name just a few of the more recent winners. The MVP has gone to pitchers only 16 times out of the 99 awards given since 1931. Vass goes on to add that, in the 23 years since the inception of the Cy Young Award in 1956, only five pitchers have won the MVP. The problem is that one set of writers from the BBWA votes for the MVPs and another, different set votes for the Cy Young awards. Presumably, most of the MVP voters feel that a pitcher will or should get the Cy Young if he had such a good year. Therefore, they do not vote for pitchers for MVP.

In the 1970s, only one pitcher won the MVP, and to do that he had to pile up a 24–8 record, with 301 strikeouts and a league-leading 1.82 ERA.

Pitchers have been overlooked so many times for the MVP award that some, such as Ron Guidry, say that either it should be renamed the Most Valuable Player Except for Pitchers Award or that there should be a separate award, other than the Cy Young, perhaps the Most Valuable Pitcher Award. When one looks at Guidry's league-leading stats of 25–3 and an ERA of 1.74 in 1974 and considers that the MVP went to Jim Rice that year, one begins to understand the pitchers' point of view.

Another source of controversy is what I call the "front-runner syndrome," the tendency to give preference to that player whose team finished high in the standings. In the 1970s, only two players won MVPs who were on teams that finished lower than second in their divisions. One of these players was Rod Carew (1977) who won his sixth AL batting championship that year, and the second was Keith Hernandez (1979). Hernandez led the NL with a .344 batting average, 116 runs, and 48 doubles. He also had 210 hits and 105 RBIs.

There is no clear agreement as to precisely what being "most valuable" really means. Many say that it should go to the player without whom the club would not have performed as well or placed as high. This argument holds that a .350 hitter for a last-place team should not be considered valuable to his team because they would have finished last without him.

Proponents of this theory obviously cast enough votes for Willie Stargell to place him in a tie with Keith Hernandez for MVP in 1979. Stargell was the highly touted leader of the World Champion Pirates that year, but he did not place in the top ten in the league in the major offensive categories. Could Pittsburgh have gone all the way without his physical leadership, perhaps his spiritual or psychological leadership as well? Probably not.

Ironically, Stargell felt that he should have won the MVP over Joe Torre in 1971, just because the Pirates came in first and Torre's Cards came in second. He felt this in spite of the fact that Torre outhit him .363 to .295 and had more RBIs as well.

As evidence that the controversy remains, please consider that, in 1979, not one first-place vote was cast for players such as Pete

Rose, Dave Parker, Dave Concepcion, Dave Kingman, George Foster, Mike Schmidt, and so on. This is not necessarily a bad thing, until you consider that a first-place vote was actually cast for Gary Carter and another first-place vote was cast for Bill Madlock. Carter hit .283 and had 75 RBIs for Montreal, and Bill Madlock hit .298 and had 85 RBIs for San Francisco and Pittsburgh. Both had perfectly respectable years, but they were hardly of MVP quality.

As controversial as the MVP Award may be and as many inequities as it may have, it is still one of baseball's premier honors. The MVPs of the 1970s will take their place in history to be argued about in the Hot Stove League for decades to come. Among the many oddities and distinctions will remain the fact that Reggie Jackson was a unanimous choice for MVP and, in achieving this, he stands next to the seven unanimous choices who preceded him: Babe Ruth, Hank Greenberg, Al Rosen, Mickey Mantle, Frank Robinson, Orlando Cepeda, and Denny McLain.

The MVP quiz is Q and A and multiple choice.

QUIZ 1

1. Which two players did *not* win two MVPs each in the 1970s?
   a. Steve Garvey
   b. Johnny Bench
   c. Pete Rose
   d. Joe Morgan
2. Which two NL players who won MVPs also led the league in RBIs *and* home runs in the same season?
3. Who are the two Oakland A's who won AL MVPs in the 1970s?
4. Who won the NL MVP in the one year in the 1970s in which a player for Cincinnati, St. Louis, or Pittsburgh did not win it?
5. Johnny Bench won the NL MVP in 1970. Who was the last player for the Reds to achieve that honor?
6. Who are the two Red Sox players named as MVPs in the 1970s?
7. Rod Carew won the AL MVP in 1977. Who was the last player for the Twins to achieve that honor?
8. No player won the AL MVP in consecutive years in the 1970s. Who was the last player, a Yankee, to do so?
9. Batting average obviously has a lot to do with the choice of an MVP, because, in the NL, the batting champion was also named MVP four times in the 1970s. Who were the four players to win both honors?

10. There also seems to be a high correlation between home-run production and the MVP award, because the same player won both in the same year in both leagues three times. Who are the NL players and the AL players who led the league in home runs and won the MVP the same year in the 1970s?

Quiz 1—Answers

1. a and c
2. George Foster led in both in 1977, and Johnny Bench led in both in 1970, and both won MVPs.
3. Vida Blue in 1971, and Reggie Jackson in 1973.
4. Steve Garvey of the Dodgers won it in 1974.
5. Frank Robinson was the last Red to win it, in 1961. He was also the only man to win it in both leagues.
6. Jim Rice in 1978, and Fred Lynn in 1975. Yaz was MVP in 1967.
7. Harmon Killebrew was the last Twin to win it, in 1969.
8. The last player to win back-to-back MVPs was Roger Maris in 1960 and 1961. Mickey Mantle also accomplished the same feat, but that was in 1956 and 1957.
9. The four players are: Joe Torre (1971), Pete Rose (1973), Dave Parker (1978), and Keith Hernandez (1979).
10. In the NL, Bench won both honors in 1970 and 1973, and George Foster also won both in 1977.

    In the AL, it was Dick Allen in 1972, Reggie Jackson in 1973, and Jim Rice in 1978.

GOLD GLOVES

It is an aphorism among military strategists and tacticians that "the best defense is a good offense." In the three major team sports—baseball, basketball, and football—today, almost the reverse is true. Greater and greater emphasis is being placed on the Big D. Basketball players are judged not only on how many points they score but also on how many points they allow the opposing player to score. From Pop Warner to the pros, football stadiums resound with the repeated plea of "Dee-fense, dee-fense." And in baseball, even with the designated-hitter rule in effect in the AL, very few teams can afford to keep a man on the roster who has a big stick but no glove.

The Rawlings Sporting Goods Company, in conjunction with *The Sporting News,* established the Gold Glove Award in 1957. That first year, one major-league team was selected by a group of 19 sportswriters. The next year, an all-star fielding team in each league was selected by a poll of the players. From 1964 to 1975, this was changed to a vote by managers and coaches. From 1975 through 1977, the 26 major-league managers, the top broadcasters from each club, and a feature writer from *The Sporting News* made the selections. In 1978 and 1979, selections were again made by the managers and coaches.

Although there is some correlation between the number of Gold Gloves a club won in the 1970s and the success that team achieved during the same period, that correlation is not as high as one might have expected. Throughout the 1970s, Baltimore was ahead of all other AL teams with 29 Gold Glove awards, and Cincinnati led all NL teams with 25. This is just about what one would have expected, given the fact that Baltimore and Cincinnati were league champions, three times and four times respectively. But Pittsburgh, twice the NL champion, is represented with only 6 Gold Glove awards, trailing well behind Philadelphia's 16, Los Angeles' 13, Houston's 11, and St. Louis's 7.

The Oakland A's won only three Gold Gloves in the 1970s, and only one of those during the three consecutive years when they were World Champions. That one award went to Joe Rudi in 1975. In the two years when the Cincinnati Reds were World Champions, they had four Gold Glove winners. These apparent contradictions and correlations help to emphasize that many different kinds of skills are needed to put together a winning team. Defense, by itself, is not enough.

Since the voting is conducted just prior to the end of the season, the award does not always go to the player with the highest fielding percentage for the year. Of the four AL infielders with the best fielding averages in 1979, for example, only one (Rick Burleson) was voted a Gold Glove. Some subjectivity must come into play in choosing outfielders also, because it is obviously not done on strictly quantitative lines. Many would argue, for example, that Rupert Jones was a better outfielder in 1979 than Sixto Lezcano was, but the latter won a Gold Glove and the former did not.

In the NL, in 1979, the top fielding percentages, by position, for infielders, were held by Willie Stargell, Ken Oberkfell, Ron Cey, and Larry Bowa. Indeed, Bowa's .991 fielding percentage led the league and set a new major-league record. The Gold Glove for the NL shortstop went to Dave Concepcion, who committed 27 errors to Bowa's 6. However, the award is given for overall fielding excellence, not just the highest fielding percentage, and Concepcion did make more putouts; he also had more assists, and he turned half again as many double plays.

The other Gold Gloves for the NL infield did not go to Stargell, Oberkfell, and Cey, but rather to Keith Hernandez, Manny Trillo, and Mike Schmidt.

Whatever the complaints about the shortcomings or inequities of this annual award may be, it helps to emphasize the importance of defensive skills and it honors 18 men—the men with the Gold Gloves.

Gold Gloves quizzes are Q and A and multiple choice.

QUIZ 1

1. What pitcher won Gold Gloves in both leagues?
   a. Phil Niekro
   b. Jim Kaat
   c. Nolan Ryan
   d. Ferguson Jenkins
2. Who were the three third basemen who won the Gold Gloves in the four years in the 1970s in which Brooks Robinson did not win?
   a. Buddy Bell, Carney Lansford, and Sal Bando
   b. Graig Nettles, Buddy Bell, and Aurelio Rodriguez
   c. Sal Bando, Doug De Cinces, and Toby Harrah
   d. Graig Nettles, George Brett, and Carney Lansford
3. Which one of the following AL infielders did *not* win a Gold Glove in the 1970s?
   a. Bobby Grich
   b. Willie Randolph
   c. Chris Chambliss
   d. Luis Aparicio
4. Which one of the following NL outfielders did *not* win a Gold Glove in the 1970s?
   a. Bobby Bonds
   b. Cesar Cedeno
   c. Roberto Clemente
   d. Dusty Baker
5. Richie Allen, Boog Powell, Pete Rose, Keith Hernandez—how many of these MVPs won Gold Gloves in the 1970s?
   a. 1
   b. 2
   c. 3
   d. 4
6. Which one of these AL players did *not* win Gold Gloves in successive years?
   a. Dave Johnson
   b. Paul Blair
   c. Graig Nettles
   d. Jim Spencer
7. Two NL teams won only one Gold Glove each in the 1970s. Which of the following combinations of teams is correct?
   a. New York and Pittsburgh
   b. San Francisco and Montreal
   c. Atlanta and Houston
   d. Chicago and San Diego
8. Vida Blue, Jim Palmer, Ron Guidry, Mike Flanagan—how many of these Cy Young Award winners did *not* win a Gold Glove in the 1970s?
   a. 1
   b. 2
   c. 3
   d. 4

9. One AL team had four Gold Glove winners in each of four different years. Name the team.
10. Name the players.

QUIZ 2

1. Which of these catchers won the Gold Glove the most times in the 1970s?
   a. Carlton Fisk c. Jim Sundberg
   b. Thurman Munson d. Ray Fosse
2. Which one of the following AL outfielders did *not* win a Gold Glove in the 1970s?
   a. Bobby Murcer c. Chet Lemon
   b. Paul Blair d. Amos Otis
3. Which one of the following NL infielders did *not* win a Gold Glove in the 1970s?
   a. Felix Millan c. Ron Cey
   b. Dave Concepcion d. Mike Schmidt
4. Tom Seaver, Steve Carlton, Bruce Sutter, Ferguson Jenkins—how many of these NL Cy Young Award winners did *not* win a Gold Glove in the 1970s?
   a. 1 c. 3
   b. 2 d. 4
5. Which of these NL players did *not* win Gold Gloves in successive years?
   a. Pete Rose c. Cesar Cedeno
   b. Willie Davis d. Cesar Geronimo
6. Four AL teams won only three Gold Gloves each in the 1970s. Which of the following combinations of teams is correct?
   a. Oakland, California, Cleveland, and Minnesota
   b. Texas, Detroit, Chicago, and Oakland
   c. Oakland, California, Texas, and Detroit
   d. Cleveland, Minnesota, Texas, and Detroit
7. Which of the following teams did Jim Kaat play for when he won his Gold Gloves in the 1970s?
   a. Milwaukee, Detroit, St. Louis
   b. Minnesota, Chicago, Philadelphia
   c. Detroit, Philadelphia, Houston
   d. Cleveland, Chicago, Montreal

8. Which one of these players did *not* win at least five Gold Gloves in the 1970s?
   a. George Scott
   b. Steve Garvey
   c. Joe Morgan
   d. Mark Belanger
9. One NL team had the same four men win Gold Gloves in four different years in the 1970s. Name the team.
10. Name the players.

Quiz 1—Answers

1. b
2. b
3. b
4. d
5. b. Rose and Hernandez won Gold Gloves.
6. d
7. d
8. c. Jim Palmer won a Gold Glove in 1979.
9. Baltimore
10. In 1971, Baltimore had Dave Johnson at second, Brooks Robinson at third, Mark Belanger at short, and Paul Blair in the outfield. Johnson, Belanger, and Blair repeated in 1973, 1974, and 1975, and they were joined in those three years by Bobby Grich at second.

Quiz 2—Answers

1. c. Sundberg won it four times (1976–80), while Fosse won twice (1970–71), Fisk once (1972), and Munson three times (1973–75).
2. c
3. c
4. d
5. a
6. a
7. b
8. b
9. Cincinnati
10. Johnny Bench was the catcher, Joe Morgan the second baseman, Dave Concepcion the shortstop, and Cesar Geronimo was in the outfield, from 1974 through 1977.

STEALING

Speed, particularly on the base paths, is, along with pitching, hitting, and fielding, one of the essentials of a winning team. A fast runner on base makes everyone start thinking, and, as Yogi Berra has pointed out, mistakes begin to happen when everyone starts thinking. A speedy runner on base means that the pitcher has to use some of his concentration, better directed toward the batter, in order to keep the runner close to the base; the infielders have to check their signals to be sure who will hold the runner to the bag and who will cover in the event of an attempted steal; the catcher must be cautious about the pitches he calls; the outfielders have to play the ball differently to keep the runner from taking the extra base.

The stolen base, or even the threat of or attempt at a stolen base, is one of the most thrilling plays in baseball. Anything can happen, and often does.

Whenever stolen bases are mentioned, the old-time fan starts talking about Jackie Robinson. Although it was a rare treat to watch the great Robinson rattle the opposing team whenever he got on the base paths, it must be remembered that he stole only 197 bases in his all too brief career of ten years, even though he led the league twice. Many other fans reach back into baseball history and celebrate the exploits of Ty Cobb and his flashing spikes. We are told that "they don't make them as good and as dedicated and as mean as The Georgia Peach anymore."

Without detracting in any way from the memory of such great ballplayers as Robinson and Cobb, and, for that matter, Bob Bescher, Clyde Milan, Eddie Collins, and Fritz Maisel, just to name a few, the truth of the matter is that the players today are just as good and just as dedicated as they ever were. As far as the other matter goes, no one ever stole a base just by being mean and flashing his spikes around.

"The Georgia Peach" stole his last base in 1928, and it was not until 1962 that Maury Wills broke Cobb's season record, established in 1915. It took the decade of the 1970s for Lou Brock to break that record again, surpassing Wills's achievement, not just by a little bit but by 14 bases. Brock also broke Cobb's "unbeatable" record of almost 900 stolen bases in a career.

The next few pages will give you the chance to brush up on your knowledge of the 1970s as it applies to one particular skill, what is mistakenly called a lost art: the art of stealing a base.

Stealing quizzes are true/false and multiple choice.

QUIZ 1

1. One of the four players below did *not* lead the NL in stolen bases in any one year. Which one was he?
   a. Davey Lopes c. Bill North
   b. Omar Moreno d. Frank Taveras
2. Which of these four players has *not* stolen over 200 bases in his career?
   a. Pat Kelly c. Reggie Jackson
   b. Toby Harrah d. Rod Carew
3. Which one of the following NL teams did *not* have a player lead the league in stolen bases in the 1970s?
   a. St. Louis c. Montreal
   b. Los Angeles d. Pittsburgh
4. Which one of these four players has stolen the most bases in his career?
   a. Bobby Bonds c. Cesar Cedeno
   b. Amos Otis d. Joe Morgan
5. Which one of these four players led the major leagues in stolen bases in the 1979 season?
   a. Bump Wills c. Keith Hernandez
   b. Willie Wilson d. Omar Moreno
6. Which one of the following players did *not* lead the NL in base stealing two years in a row?

a. Davey Lopes
b. Omar Moreno
c. Frank Taveras
d. Lou Brock

7. Which one of the following players does *not* hold a team record for most bases stolen in his career?
   a. Toby Harrah
   b. Rod Carew
   c. Henry Aaron
   d. Joe Morgan
8. Which of the following players is within 250 stolen bases of Brock's career record?
   a. Ron Le Flore
   b. Bert Campaneris
   c. Joe Morgan
   d. Bobby Bonds
9. Lou Brock broke Maury Wills's record for stolen bases in one season. Which of the combinations below is Wills's old record and Brock's new one?
   a. 104–118
   b. 108–118
   c. 114–120
   d. 118–120
10. Answer the following statements true or false.
    a. Henry Aaron and Rod Carew hold the career records for stolen bases for the Braves and the Twins.
    b. At least six players still active at the end of the 1979 season have stolen 500 or more bases.
    c. In 1979, Lee Mazzilli stole more bases than Billy North did.
    d. Carl Yastrzemski stole more than 200 bases in his career.

QUIZ 2

1. Which one of the following players was *not* caught stealing at least 20 times in 1979?
   a. Terry Puhl
   b. Ivan DeJesus
   c. Pete Rose
   d. Bobby Bonds
2. Which one of the following players has stolen the most bases in his career?
   a. Reggie Smith
   b. Dave Winfield
   c. Jose Cardenal
   d. Claudell Washington
3. Which one of the following players has stolen the fewest bases in his career?
   a. Dave Concepcion
   b. Mickey Rivers
   c. Larry Bowa
   d. Reggie Jackson

4. The four players listed below led the major leagues in career stolen bases among all active players at the end of the 1970s. Which one of the four has the highest average per season?
   a. Bert Campaneris　　c. Bobby Bonds
   b. Joe Morgan　　d. Cesar Cedeno
5. In the 1970s, which NL player came the closest to Lou Brock's 118 stolen bases in one season?
   a. Frank Taveras with 57　　c. Davey Lopes with 77
   b. Bobby Tolan with 67　　d. Omar Moreno with 77
6. Which one of the following players leads the major leagues in the total of home runs and stolen bases?
   a. Reggie Jackson　　c. Bert Campaneris
   b. Joe Morgan　　d. Bobby Bonds
7. Only one of the players below has a total of more than 500 home runs and stolen bases. Which one is he?
   a. Jose Cardenal　　c. Carl Yastrzemski
   b. Mike Schmidt　　d. Freddie Patek
8. Which one of the following players has the highest total of home runs and stolen bases?
   a. Bobby Bonds　　c. Carl Yastrzemski
   b. Reggie Jackson　　d. Jose Cardenal
9. Which one of the following players has the lowest total of home runs and stolen bases?
   a. Amos Otis　　c. Dave Winfield
   b. Bobby Murcer　　d. Mike Schmidt
10. Answer the following statements true or false.
    a. When Brock led the NL in stolen bases in 1971, 1972, 1973, and 1974, he averaged over 75 stolen bases a season.
    b. Joe Morgan stole more bases in his career than Maury Wills did.
    c. Fred Patek stole more bases in his career than Frankie Frisch did.
    d. Ty Cobb stole more bases in his best year than Carl Yastrzemski did in his first 19 years in the majors.

Quiz 1—Answers

1. c
2. b. The numbers are Kelly 232, Harrah 160, Jackson 211, and Carew 289.

3. c. St. Louis had Lou Brock; Los Angeles had Davey Lopes; Pittsburgh had both Frank Taveras and Omar Moreno.
4. d. Morgan stole 601, as compared to Bonds's 441, Otis's 295, and Cedeno's 427.
5. b. Wilson stole 83, as compared to Bump Wills's 35, Hernandez's 11, and Moreno's 77.
6. c. Taveras led the league once, in 1977, with 70 stolen bases.
7. d
8. Sorry to trick you, but no active player was within 250 of Brock's career record of 938 as of the end of the 1979 season.
9. a. Wills set his record in 1962, and Brock broke it in 1974.
10. a. True
    b. False. Only Campaneris and Morgan are in this category.
    c. False. North stole 58 bases to Mazzilli's 34.
    d. False. Yaz stole 168 bases in the first 19 years of his career.

Quiz 2—Answers

1. c. Pete Rose was caught stealing only 11 times. Puhl was caught 22 times, DeJesus 20 times, and Bonds 23 times.
2. c. Cardenal stole 329 bases, as compared to Smith's 125, Winfield's 110, and Washington's 128.
3. d. Reggie Jackson has stolen 211 bases, as compared to Concepcion's 220, Rivers's 226, and Bowa's 251.
4. d. Cedeno's average of 42.7 (427 stolen bases in ten years) is highest. Campaneris's is 39.25 (628 in 16), Morgan's is 35.35 (601 in 17), and Bonds's is 36.75 (441 in 12).
5. c and d. Davey Lopes and Omar Moreno came the closest. Lopes stole 77 bases in 1975, and Moreno stole the same amount in 1979. Taveras actually stole 70 in 1977, and Tolan led the league with 57 stolen bases in 1970.
6. b. Morgan leads both leagues with a total of 814 (213 home runs and 601 stolen bases).
7. c. Yaz has a total of 572 (404 home runs and 168 stolen bases).
8. a. Bonds not only leads these four, but he is second only to Joe Morgan in this category. His total is 761 (321 home runs and 440 stolen bases), as compared to Reggie Jackson's 580 (369 home runs and 211 stolen bases), Yaz's 572 (see #7 above), and Cardenal's 467 (138 home runs and 329 stolen bases).
9. c. Dave Winfield's total is 244 (134 home runs and 110 stolen

bases), as compared to Otis's 454 (159 home runs and 295 stolen bases), Murcer's 348 (225 home runs and 123 stolen bases), and Schmidt's 352 (235 home runs and 117 stolen bases).

10. a. True. He stole a total of 315 bases for an average, in those four years, of 78.75 stolen bases per season.
    b. True. He stole 601 to Maury Wills's 586.
    c. False. He stole 377 to Frankie Frisch's 419.
    d. False. Yaz stole 168 bases, and Cobb's best year was 1915, when he stole 96 bases.

BASE-STEALING DUOS

When one speaks of the great duos in baseball, the conversation is usually about a pair of great hitters, often back to back in the lineup. The names of Roger Maris and Mickey Mantle, Babe Ruth and Lou Gehrig, and Hack Wilson and Gabby Hartnett are the ones that most often come to mind.

Although base stealing is usually thought of as a one-man effort, it too has had its great duos throughout history. Going into the 1970s, the greatest pair on the base paths were Clyde Milan and Danny Moeller of the Senators, who stole a record 137 bases between them in 1913. The modern equivalent of that mercurial pair was Maury Wills and Willie Davis, who stole 136 bases between them in 1962 with the Dodgers.

Ty Cobb belonged to two duos who stole 100 bases or more in one season five different times: four times with Donie Bush and once with Sam Crawford. Frank Chance and Johnny Evers, two-thirds of the famous trio of Tinker to Evers to Chance, stole 106 bases between them in 1906 with the Cubs. Chance had also teamed up with Jimmy Slagle to steal 100 in 1903.

In the 1970s, however, a new pair came along and shattered all the records set before them. Indeed, of all the duos who stole 100 or more bases between them in one season, fully one-third of them performed that feat in the 1970s.

These 11 pairs are listed on the opposite page. Bring all your memory and knowledge to bear on these four columns and match the combined number of bases stolen in one season with the pair of players and finally with their team and the year in which they did it.

Number of Bases Stolen	*Pair of Base Stealers*	*Team*	*Year*
148	Amos Otis, Fred Patek	Reds	1972
129	Omar Moreno, Frank Taveras	Cardinals	1976
123	Joe Morgan, Bobby Tolan	Athletics	1975
117	Lou Brock, Bake McBride	Pirates	1971
113	Willie Wilson, Amos Otis	Pirates	1974
109	Joe Morgan, Dave Concepcion	Royals	1979
105	Mickey Rivers, Jerry Remy	Pirates	1978
104	Cesar Cedeno, Jose Cruz	Angels	1977
101	Omar Moreno, Bill Madlock	Astros	1975
100	Frank Taveras, Omar Moreno	Royals	1979
100	Billy North, Bert Campaneris	Reds	1977

Stealing Duos—Answers

Number of Bases Stolen	*Pair of Base Stealers*	*Team*	*Year*
148	Lou Brock (118), Bake McBride (30)	Cardinals	1974
129	Billy North (75), Bert Campaneris (54)	Athletics	1976
123	Frank Taveras (70), Omar Moreno (53)	Pirates	1977
117	Omar Moreno (71), Frank Taveras (46)	Pirates	1978
113	Willie Wilson (83), Amos Otis (30)	Royals	1979
109	Omar Moreno (77), Bill Madlock (32)	Pirates	1979
105	Cesar Cedeno (61), Jose Cruz (44)	Astros	1977
104	Mickey Rivers (70), Jerry Remy (34)	Angels	1975
101	Amos Otis (52), Fred Patek (49)	Royals	1971
100	Joe Morgan (58), Bobby Tolan (42)	Reds	1972
100	Joe Morgan (67), Dave Concepcion (33)	Reds	1975

ROOKIE OF THE YEAR

In 1971, the Official Major League Scoring Committee, at the request of the BBWA, changed the definition of a rookie to a player who did not have more than 130 at-bats or 50 innings pitched in the major leagues during a previous season or seasons, nor more than 45 days on a major-league roster during the 25-player limit from the start of the season to August 31 (excluding time in military service).

In baseball, as in life, hope springs eternal. While most of North America is still digging out from the snows of winter, spring training camps in Florida, Arizona, and California are opening with expectations that the season to come will be the one when the team finally puts it all together and captures a World Championship. Every team expects that, among the many hundreds of fresh-faced youngsters who appear in spring training, there will be at least one or two players who will help them, who will fill a weak spot on the roster or back up an aging veteran.

Every owner, coach, and manager also dares to hope, to dream, to pray that among the new crop of rookies is that one player, that one superstar of the future who will pack the stands with fans and who will carry the club to new heights.

Somewhere among all those rookies are the two players who will be named Rookie of the Year. Somewhere among them may be a Willie Mays, a Willie McCovey, a Tom Seaver, a Johnny Bench, a Pete Rose, or a Rod Carew, to name just a few previous winners of this award.

The Baseball Writers Association of America (BBWA) started voting for the Rookie of the Year in 1947. The first two years, they made just one selection: Jackie Robinson the first year and Alvin Dark in 1948. Since then they have chosen one Rookie of the Year from each league every year, with the exception of the two occasions (1976 and 1979) on which they had tie votes and two players were chosen.

There were many prodigious, indeed, virtually unbeatable records set by rookies before the BBWA began their award. In pitching, consider the 28–13 record posted by Grover Cleveland Alexander in 1911 and the 12 wins in a row of George Wiltse in 1904 and Atley Donald in 1939. In batting, consider Joe DiMaggio's debut in 1936 as he set the rookie records of 132 runs and a league-leading 15 triples. Only two years later, "The Splendid Splinter," Ted Williams, burst to stardom with rookie records of 149 bases on balls, a .609 slugging average, and 149 RBIs.

Among the other records set by rookies since 1947, when the award began, the following should be noted: Karl Spooner's 15 strikeouts in his first game in 1954 (a feat previously accomplished by Bob Feller in his debut in 1936), Herb Score's 245 strikeouts in 1955, Frank Robinson's 38 home runs in 1956, and Jerry Koosman's seven shutouts in 1968.

Some years have been remarkably better than others, and 1964 was one of the better years for rookies. The Rookie of the Year in the AL was Minnesota's Tony Oliva, who set first-year records with 217 hits and 374 total bases. Dick Allen of the Phillies set the NL rookie record with 353 total bases.

The 1970 selections of Rookie of the Year provide an interesting number of records, firsts, and unique features. Until the 1970s, only four pitchers had been selected a Rookie of the Year in the NL. They were: Don Newcombe in 1949, Joe Black in 1952, Jack Sanford in 1957, and Tom Seaver in 1967. After choosing only these four pitchers in 23 years, the BBWA went on to name six pitchers in the NL in one ten-year span. In the same period, only one rookie pitcher won the award in the AL.

It is interesting to note that the drought of great rookie catchers ended in the 1970s. Johnny Bench was the only catcher in either league to be named Rookie of the Year between 1947 and 1970. The new decade soon saw Atlanta's Earl Williams named in 1971. The AL, which never had a catcher named Rookie of the Year, soon had two: Thurman Munson and Carlton Fisk. Munson was named in 1970 and Fisk in 1972.

Of these three catchers, Williams moved around to several clubs and had a respectable but not outstanding record before retiring. Munson went on to stardom as the first Yankee captain since Lou Gehrig, and he was the MVP of the AL in 1976. Many feel that he would have carved out a niche for himself at Cooperstown had it not been for the airplane accident that so tragically ended his life in 1979. Fisk played through the 1970s with the Red Sox and, at the end of the decade, was recognized as outstanding at his craft, with a special talent for handling young pitchers, and a solid .284 career batting average as well.

Fred Lynn hit the major leagues in 1975, and he became the first man in history to be named both Rookie of the Year and MVP in the same year. He played in 145 games, and he had a .331 batting average, with 21 home runs and 105 RBIs. One of the rookies whom Lynn narrowly edged out was his teammate, Jim Rice. George Vass, *Baseball Digest*'s chronicler of rookies, observed at the time, "Not since Luke Easter and Al Rosen came up at the same time with Cleveland twenty-five years ago has a team had the good fortune to have two such power-hitting rookies appear together."

Not every Rookie of the Year goes on to find that his star has found a permanent place in the firmament. Many shoot their light across the sky for a year or two and lapse into obscurity. A recent example is the unfortunate case of Mark Fidrych.

Anyone who ever saw his head of long blond curly hair atop a gangling 6′3″ body and the awkward good looks of a 21-year-old would not long wonder why a teammate, obviously a "Sesame Street" watcher, gave him his nickname, "The Bird." He went to the Detroit training camp as a nonroster player, but he soon caught the eye of manager Ralph Houk. Houk put him on the team and gave him his first starting assignment on May 15, 1976, against the Cleveland Indians. Fidrych pitched a two-hitter, and his storybook romance with baseball fans everywhere was under way.

This unassuming, unspoiled young man caught everyone's attention with what many considered to be eccentricities at best. He crawled around the mound, smoothing out spike marks; he applauded his outfielders for their catches; and he was known to run over and shake an infielder's hand after a good play. The Bird's unabashed exuberance excited crowd and teammates alike.

At the end of the season, he had won 19 games and lost only 9. He led the league with 24 complete games and a 2.34 ERA, and he was named Rookie of the Year by the BBWA and Rookie Pitcher of the Year by *The Sporting News*. He had earned his annual salary of $16,500.

In 1977, his record slipped to 6–4, and chronic arm problems kept him on the disabled list for much of the year. It was worse in 1978. Even though he won two and lost none with Detroit, he was again on the disabled list, and he was sent down to the Lakeland club in the Florida State League. The 1979 statistics are shocking and sad. Fidrych gave up 23 hits in 15 innings, posting a 0–3 record and an ERA of 10.20.

By the end of the decade, it looked like the end of the road for this fresh young star who, as a rookie, had captured the imagination of his fans and inspired his team as few had done before him.

The newness and eagerness of spring soon become the dog days of summer and, eventually, the falling leaves of October.

Rookie of the Year quizzes are Q and A and multiple choice.

QUIZ 1

1. Only one player in history won Rookie of the Year honors and the MVP Award in the same year. Who was he?
2. 1976 saw the only tie in Rookie of the Year voting in NL history. Who were the players who tied?
3. In 1974, the Rangers became the first AL team since the 1962 Yankees (Mantle and Tresh), and the only AL team in the 1970s to have an MVP and a Rookie of the Year in the same year. The MVP was Jeff Burroughs. Who was the rookie?
4. Which NL team did *not* have a Rookie of the Year in the 1970s?
   a. Padres   c. Mets
   b. Pirates   d. Expos
5. Three teams in the AL had Rookies of the Year *twice* in the 1970s. Which of these four combinations were they?
   a. Yankees, Twins, Orioles   c. Orioles, Red Sox, Tigers
   b. Indians, Red Sox, Twins   d. Oakland, Yankees, Orioles
6. In the 1970s, six NL pitchers won Rookie of the Year honors,

as compared to one pitcher in the AL. How many of the six can you name?

7. Of these six pitchers, who won the most games in the year he was Rookie of the Year?
8. Of these six pitchers, who had the lowest ERA in the year he was Rookie of the Year?
9. Which was the only NL team to have different players win both the Cy Young Award and Rookie of the Year in the same year in the 1970s?
10. Which of the following NL Rookies of the Year had the highest batting average in the year in which he won?
    a. Gary Matthews c. Andre Dawson
    b. Bake McBride d. Bob Horner

QUIZ 2

1. One player in the 1970s won the Rookie of the Year Award and went on to win an MVP also. Who was he?
2. 1979 saw the only tie in Rookie of the Year voting in AL history. Who were the players who tied?
3. In 1976, the Reds became the first NL team since the 1953 Dodgers (Campanella and Gilliam) and the only NL team in the 1970s to have an MVP and a Rookie of the Year in the same year. The MVP was Joe Morgan. Who was the rookie?
4. Which AL team did *not* have a Rookie of the Year in the 1970s?
    a. Indians c. Angels
    b. Blue Jays d. Twins
5. Who was the only unanimous selection in the 1970s for Rookie of the Year?
6. In the 1970s, only one AL pitcher won Rookie of the Year honors. In what important category did he lead the league?
7. Which of the following AL Rookies of the Year had the highest batting average in the year in which he won?
    a. Chris Chambliss c. Al Bumbry
    b. Carlton Fisk d. John Castino
8. Three teams in the NL had Rookies of the Year *twice* in the 1970s. Which one of these four combinations were they?
    a. Dodgers, Reds, Giants c. Padres, Expos, Cubs
    b. Expos, Braves, Giants d. Phillies, Dodgers, Braves

9. Which was the only AL team to have different players win both the Cy Young Award and Rookie of the Year honors in the same year in the 1970s?
10. Who were the three players from Canadian teams to win Rookie of the Year honors in the 1970s?

Quiz 1—Answers

1. Fred Lynn hit .331 in 1975, while leading the league with 103 runs and 47 doubles. He also hit 21 home runs and had 105 RBIs.
2. Pat Zachry of the Reds and Butch Metzger of the Padres each received 11 votes.
3. The rookie was Mike Hargrove, who hit .323.
4. b. The Pirates have not had a Rookie of the Year since the BBWA began giving the award.
5. c. The Orioles had Al Bumbry and Eddie Murray; the Red Sox had Carlton Fisk and Fred Lynn; the Tigers had Mark Fidrych and Lou Whitaker.
6. The six NL pitchers were: Carl Morton (Montreal), Jon Matlack (New York), John Montefusco (San Francisco), Butch Metzger (San Diego), Pat Zachry (Cincinnati), and Rick Sutcliffe (Los Angeles).
7. Carl Morton was 18–11 in 1970.
8. Matlack had an ERA of 2.32.
9. San Diego's Randy Jones won the Cy Young and Butch Metzger tied for Rookie of the Year honors in 1976.
10. b. McBride hit .309, compared to Matthews's .300, Dawson's .282, and Horner's .266.

Quiz 2—Answers

1. Thurman Munson was Rookie of the Year in 1970 and MVP in 1976.
2. Alfredo Griffin of the Blue Jays and John Castino of the Twins each received seven votes.
3. The rookie was Pat Zachry, who had a 14–7 record and a 2.74 ERA.
4. c. The California Angels have not yet had a Rookie of the Year.
5. Carlton Fisk received 24 votes in 1972. He hit .293, with 22

home runs and 61 RBIs. He also led the league with nine triples. Fisk was the only unanimous choice in the AL since the awards began.

6. Mark Fidrych led the league with a 2.34 ERA. He also had a 19–9 record in 1976.
7. Al Bumbry hit .337 in 1973, as compared to Fisk's .293, Castino's .285, and Chambliss's .275.
8. b. The Expos had Carl Morton and Andre Dawson; the Braves had Earl Williams and Bob Horner; the Giants had Gary Matthews and John Montefusco.
9. Baltimore's Jim Palmer won the Cy Young Award, and Al Bumbry was Rookie of the Year in 1973.
10. The three players were: Carl Morton (Montreal Expos, 1970), Andre Dawson (Montreal Expos, 1977), and John Castino (Toronto Blue Jays, 1979).

ALL-STAR GAME

Arch Ward, sports editor of the *Chicago Tribune,* is generally regarded as the father of baseball's All-Star game. Although he was certainly not the first man to have such an idea, he was the one who thought of it as a special event for Chicago's Century of Progress Exposition, commemorating the 100th anniversary of the city's founding. He was also the man who sold it to the first commissioner of baseball, Judge Kenesaw Mountain Landis, as well as to the owners of the clubs.

The fear of injury to a star and the assumption that a midseason All-Star game would, in some way, detract from the World Series were but two of the reasons why the owners then insisted that the game be on a one-time basis only.

Still another reason was that the whole idea of "all-stars" was generally regarded as bush, nothing more than barnstorming commercialism. Since the major leagues consisted of only 16 teams in 11 cities, and since there was no TV to offer national exposure, most of the United States survived on minor-league baseball, and they were very eager to see the stars whom they read about in the newspapers. It was customary for players such as Babe Ruth and Lou Gehrig to assemble teams and tour the South and the West in the off-season for a month or so. Not only did this give many fans the opportunity to see big-league ballplayers, but it also gave the players themselves one of their few chances to earn some extra money.

It must be remembered that ballplayers did not have the same potential for earning money in the off-season as they do now. Although it is true that some stars such as Nap Lajoie earned a few dollars by endorsing Red Devil chewing tobacco and Coca-Cola in the early 1900s, the possibilities for endorsements, commercials, and speaking engagements that exist today are not comparable in any way.

In any event, the first game was played at Comiskey Park on July 6, 1933, and it was attended by a sellout crowd of 47,595. The manager of the American League team, Connie Mack, let it be known that he was out for a win and that he was not interested in just playing a lot of stars. Except for the pitchers, he made only one change in his starting lineup. This maneuver left his bench packed with superstars such as Tony Lazzeri, Jimmie Foxx, and catchers Mickey Cochrane and Bill Dickey (Rick Ferrell caught the entire game).

John McGraw, who had retired in the middle of the 1932 season, and who was to die only seven months later, had four members of the St. Louis Cardinals team which he so despised in his starting lineup. The leaders of the Gashouse Gang, Pepper Martin and Frankie Frisch, were one and two in the batting order, and Ace Wilson and Wild Bill Hallahan comprised the battery. McGraw played 17 of the 18 men on his roster.

The star of the game was none other than Babe Ruth, whose home run with one man on base in the third inning supplied the winning edge for the American League. Nearing the end of a magnificent career, he also made one of the outstanding defensive plays by racing to catch a line drive off the bat of Hall of Famer Chick Hafey.

The game was so popular with the fans that it was played again in 1934. This time it was at the Polo Grounds, and the crowd was even larger. One of the most memorable of all feats in baseball lore occurred that July 10, and it featured that great left-hander, King Carl Hubbell of the New York Giants. With two men on base in the first inning, Hubbell struck out Babe Ruth, Lou Gehrig, and Jimmie Foxx in order. In the second inning, he fanned Al Simmons and Joe Cronin to make it five in a row. After Bill Dickey singled, Hubbell struck out the opposing pitcher, Yankee great Lefty Gomez, to make a total of six strikeouts in two innings.

This midsummer classic became an annual event, with the exception of 1959 to 1962, when two games were held each year, and

1945, when the game was not held due to the war. The eight starting players for each team were named by the fans from 1947 to 1957, at which time the choice was turned over to the managers, coaches, and players. In 1970, the present system of distributing ballots at minor- and major-league parks was instituted, and the matter has been put back into the hands of the fans, more or less as Arch Ward would have liked it. The size of the roster grew gradually from the original 18 to today's 28, as new teams were added, and now each club must be represented by at least one player.

Although football, basketball, and most recently hockey have their own all-star games, none of them has the history and drama of baseball's extravaganza and none has so captured the excitement of the fans for almost 50 years.

Marvin Miller, the executive director of the players' union, points out two facts about the All-Star game that are not well known. First, the formula whereby 60 percent of the gate and the radio and TV money went into the pension fund has not existed for years. There is no accounting for the money, and there is no way of knowing how much of the proceeds goes into the pension fund. Second, in spite of this, there is no other all-star game in any professional sport in which the participants are not paid.

In these days in which there is so much loose talk about the large salaries being paid to athletes, it would be well to remember that the players at baseball's All-Star game do not show up for money, but, calling on the pride present in every man, they go to pit their skills against the very best the game has to offer. They are there to show their teams and their fans that they are truly All-Stars.

All-Stars quizzes are Q and A.

JULY 14, 1970, RIVERFRONT STADIUM, CINCINNATI
National League 5/ American League 4
Attendance: 51,838

This was a perfect game in some ways; only two extra-inning games with no errors had been played before, and only one has been played since. The AL held a 4–1 lead going into the bottom of the ninth inning, but the NL tied it and went on to win in the bottom of the twelfth inning. The game took 3 hours and 19 minutes, tying the 14-inning game at Comiskey Park in 1950. The only extra-inning game that was longer was the 15-inning game at Anaheim in 1967, which took 3 hours and 41 minutes. It was the first game since 1957 in which the fans picked the players.

Two of the records set in this game involved the number of players used in an extra-inning All-Star game: 49 men saw action between the two clubs, and the NL used 25 players.

AL	000	001	120	000	—4
NL	000	000	103	001	—5

QUIZ 1

1. Who tied the record for most hits and most singles in one game and was named the outstanding player of the game?
2. Who was the NL catcher who hit the only home run of the game in his first All-Star at-bat?
3. Who was the outfielder from the Twins who hit a double, his third in All-Star play, tying him with five others for the record of most doubles in total All-Star games?
4. The AL used seven pitchers, tying the record for most pitchers used by one club in an extra-inning All-Star game. How many can you name?
5. Who ran for Willie McCovey in the ninth inning and went on to become the winning pitcher?
6. Who was the Angel pitcher who went on to post a 22–12 record in 1970 who got the loss for the AL?
7. Who had the dubious honor of tying the record of striking out three times in one game?
8. Pete Rose scored the winning run by knocking the ball loose on a close play at home. Who was the AL catcher?
9. Who was the Yankee who went on to win 20 games in 1970 but only pitched to one batter in this game?
10. Who drove in the winning run?
11. The winning manager hit .333 in his six All-Star appearances as a player, but he only managed once. Who was he?
12. The losing manager was making his debut in an All-Star game. Three of his team's pitchers were on the squad, but he only used one of them. Who was he?

JULY 13, 1971, TIGER STADIUM, DETROIT
American League 6/ National League 4
Attendance: 53,559

The NL jumped off to a 3–0 lead, but two home runs, each with a man on base, put the AL ahead, and they went on to win. The game snapped the NL streak of eight straight wins. It was only the sixth time that no errors were made by either club in a nine-inning game. Each club left only two men on base, setting a new record for each club and both clubs.

NL	0 2 1	0 0 0	0 1 0	— 4
AL	0 0 4	0 0 2	0 0 X	— 6

QUIZ 2

1. Who was the Oakland outfielder who pinch-hit a home run for Vida Blue, joining only eight other men who had pinch-hit home runs?
2. This was only the third All-Star game in which six home runs were hit, three by each side. How many of the six hitters can you name?
3. Three homers were hit in one inning, a feat accomplished only once before. Who hit them?
4. It was the last All-Star game for two men who still hold the records for most games played by a shortstop and by a pitcher. Who were they?
5. Dock Ellis gave up two home runs in one inning, tying a record held by seven other pitchers. How many can you name?
6. Who was the winning manager who used two of his own team's pitchers? They went four innings and gave up no runs on two hits.
7. Who was the losing manager who had spent only one year in the major leagues as a player and was in his second year of managing?
8. Who became the first player in All-Star history to hit home runs for each league?
9. Who was the Twins' first baseman who figured in two double plays in this game, tying the career All-Star record of six?

10. Who was the losing pitcher who had thrown a no-hitter the month before for the Pirates?
11. Who was the Oriole outfielder who had two of the AL's six runs and was named the game's most valuable player?
12. Who was the Tiger who joined two other pitchers who had three assists in one game?

JULY 25, 1972, ATLANTA STADIUM, ATLANTA

National League 4/ American League 3

Attendance: 53,107

The AL was ahead 3–2 going into the bottom of the ninth, but the NL tied it up and went on to win 4–3 in the tenth. It was the NL's ninth win in the last ten games and the beginning of a new winning streak of eight straight. It also made the NL 7 for 7 in extra-inning games.

This was only the fourth extra-inning game that was error-free. One of the records tied was most double plays in extra innings. Each club made two, matching the feats performed at the 1943 game at Shibe Park and the 1958 game at Memorial Stadium.

AL	0 0 1	0 0 0	0 2 0	0	— 3
NL	0 0 0	0 0 2	0 0 1	1	— 4

QUIZ 3

1. Who was the second baseman who pinch-hit for Rod Carew and joined only nine other men who pinch-hit a home run in an All-Star game?
2. Who hit a home run in his second All-Star game in a row, this one before his hometown fans?
3. Who was the Met who pitched two scoreless innings, struck out four men, and got the win for the NL?
4. Who was the Cincinnati second baseman who knocked in the winning run in the bottom of the tenth inning and was named the game's most valuable player?
5. Who was the Oriole who pitched only one-third of an inning, gave up one run, and registered the loss for the AL?
6. Who was the Astro who just missed the All-Star record for most putouts by a first baseman in an extra-inning game?

7. Who was the losing manager, who was appearing in his third straight All-Star game?
8. Who was the winning manager? He never appeared in an All-Star game in his nine years as a player, but he led his Pirates to a World Series in 1971.
9. Who was the Minnesota player who got his first hit in six All-Star games?
10. Who were the two AL second basemen who drove in all three runs?
11. Aaron hit his second All-Star home run not far from the sign noting where he had hit his 600th only a year before, and it was against the same pitcher. Who was that pitcher?
12. Why did manager Weaver pinch-hit for Rod Carew?

JULY 24, 1973, ROYALS STADIUM, KANSAS CITY
National League 7/ American League 1
Attendance: 40,849

As soon as Hank Aaron broke the 1–1 tie in the top of the third, it was all over for the AL. Bobby Bonds sparked the NL to its tenth win in the last 11 games as he went 2 for 2 (a home run and a double), drove in two, and scored one. The seven pitchers who combined for a five-hitter were among the record-setting 28 players used by the NL. The AL used 26 players, adding up to a record of 54 players used by both clubs in a nine-inning game. Nineteen players had one or more assists, and 11 men came to bat as pinch-hitters. It was the eleventh errorless All-Star game in a row for the NL.

NL	0 0 2	1 2 2	0 0 0	— 7
AL	0 1 0	0 0 0	0 0 0	— 1

QUIZ 4

1. Who was the Dodger outfielder who became the eleventh man to pinch-hit a home run?
2. Who is the Met who, in this game, tied Musial's career record of 24 All-Star games and set records for most at-bats, most hits, most triples, and most stolen bases, to name a few?

3. Each club used a record number of seven pitchers. How many of the 14 can you name?
4. Who were the three players used by the NL in setting the record for most first basemen, nine-inning game?
5. Who were the three players used by the AL in setting the record for most third basemen, nine-inning game?
6. The NL added two players of their own to set a record of five third basemen used by both clubs. Who were they?
7. Who was the St. Louis pitcher who got the win in his only All-Star game?
8. Who was the Oakland pitcher who got the loss in his only All-Star game?
9. Who was the winning manager, who played 152 games at second base for the Phillies in 1959?
10. Who was the losing manager, who spent 13 seasons as a utility infielder and outfielder with Brooklyn, Baltimore, Kansas City, and Boston?
11. Each team used two catchers. Who were they?
12. Who was the Royals outfielder who went 2 for 2 and drove in the only AL run? Who scored the lone run?

JULY 23, 1974, THREE RIVERS STADIUM, CINCINNATI
National League 7/ American League 2
Attendance: 50,706

The NL coasted to its eleventh win in the last 12 All-Star games. Steve Garvey was the star of the game, with two hits, one RBI, and one run scored. He also squelched an AL rally in the third with an excellent defensive play on a hard shot by Bobby Murcer. Garvey, the starting first baseman for the NL, was chosen by the fans as a write-in candidate, since he was not even listed on the ballot.

The NL went ahead in the fourth and kept the lead. They scored on all four AL pitchers, and tied a record by scoring in five different innings.

AL	002	000	000	—2
NL	010	210	12X	—7

QUIZ 5

1. Who was the right fielder from the Braves who was playing in his twenty-third consecutive All-Star game?
2. Who was the AL infielder who set a new record by playing on the losing club 15 times?
3. Who tied the record for most double plays, career, by a third baseman?
4. Who was the Pittsburgh pitcher making his first and last appearance, who was credited with the win?
5. Who was the Boston pitcher who got his second All-Star loss?
6. Who was the Dodger starter for the NL who went on to post a 20–6 record, the best percentage (.769) in the league?
7. The only errors in the game were made by catchers. Who were they?
8. Who was the winning manager, the second Met in four years?
9. Who was the manager who lost his second All-Star game in two years?
10. The starting pitcher for the AL had pitched two innings for the NL in the 1970 All-Star game. Who was it?
11. Who was the Cardinals' outfielder who hit the game's only home run?
12. The starting third baseman for the NL got two RBIs. Who was it?

JULY 15, 1975, COUNTY STADIUM, MILWAUKEE
National League 6/ American League 3
Attendance: 51,480

The score was tied 3–3 going into the ninth, but the National League put together a three-run attack to win its fourth in a row and its twelfth game out of the last 13.

Although nine runs were scored, the ten participating pitchers gave up only one walk, setting a new record. It was only the second game in which two batters were hit by pitches; a balk was committed in only two previous games; the NL used 7 outfielders and the AL used 6, to tie the total of 13 used in 1973; and it was only the eighth nine-inning game in which there were no double plays.

NL	0 2 1	0 0 0	0 0 3	— 6
AL	0 0 0	0 0 3	0 0 0	— 3

QUIZ 6

1. Two players whose names sound similar shared outstanding player of the game honors. One was the Met pitcher who got the win, and the other was a Cub infielder. Who were they?
2. Who was the Red Sox outfielder who became only the twelfth man in All-Star game history to pinch-hit a home run?
3. Who was the player who tied a record held by only two men: Willie Mays and Stan Musial?
4. Although nine pairs of players in All-Star history hit home runs in the same inning, only three pairs ever hit them back to back. Who were the two Dodgers who did it in this game?
5. Who were the three AL players who tied the record held by only two other teams by stealing three bases?
6. One NL player also stole a base, and that total of four stolen bases in one game tied a record set in 1934. Who was that NL player?
7. Jerry Reuss and Rich Gossage joined to establish a new record. What did they do?
8. Two left fielders, Sammy West in 1937 and Frank Robinson in 1957, accepted five chances and made five putouts in a nine-inning game. Who was the Oakland player, making his third and last appearance, who tied that record?
9. Johnny Bench tied the record of most chances accepted (ten putouts and one assist) by a catcher, which had been set in 1956. Who set it?
10. Who was the Yankee who went on to his fifth straight season of 20 or more wins but was tagged with his second All-Star loss?
11. Only four other pitchers lost two All-Star games. How many can you name?
12. Who tied Roberto Clemente's record of most sacrifice flies, total games?
13. Who struck out in his one and only at-bat as a major leaguer but set a record by winning his seventh All-Star game as a manager?
14. The losing manager played in two All-Star games himself when he was a shortstop with the Giants. Who was he?

JULY 13, 1976, VETERANS STADIUM, PHILADELPHIA
National League 7/ American League 1
Attendance: 63,974

The AL sent only 29 men to the plate as they were soundly trounced before the third-largest crowd in All-Star history. This game, helping to celebrate the American Bicentennial, also produced the third-largest gate to date: $772,346.

Five NL pitchers held the AL All-Stars to one run on only five hits. Cincinnati's George Foster drove in three runs and was named MVP of the game.

It was the NL's thirteenth win in the last 14 games and their fifth in a row.

AL	000	100	000	—1
NL	202	000	03X	—7

QUIZ 7

1. Who was the Padre who pitched the last inning of the 1975 All-Star game, started this one, and was credited with the win?
2. Who was the Rookie of the Year who started the game and got the loss?
3. Who was the Houston Astro who replaced George Foster in center field and who hit the NL's other home run?
4. Who was the Dodger pitcher making his only All-Star appearance?
5. Who homered for the AL, accounting for their lone run?
6. Who was the Yankee right-hander who served up George Foster's two-run clout?
7. Who were the three third basemen used by the NL?
8. Who was the starting outfielder from the Detroit Tigers?
9. Each team used three shortstops. How many of the six can you name?
10. The winning manager was making his third appearance of the decade as an All-Star manager. Who was he?
11. The losing manager was a journeyman catcher who managed the Red Sox for two years. Who was he?
12. Who started the game for the AL, making his first All-Star appearance as a first baseman?

JULY 19, 1977, YANKEE STADIUM, NEW YORK
National League 7/ American League 5
Attendance: 56,683

The NL jumped off to a 4–0 lead with two home runs in the first inning and another in the third. The AL fought back, but their two-run rally in the bottom of the ninth was not enough.

The starting pitcher for the AL went into the record books as the only man to give up three home runs in one All-Star game. He also joined Claude Passeau (1941), Sandalio Consuegra (1954), and Jim Maloney (1965) in allowing a record high of five earned runs in one game.

Joe Morgan tied Mickey Mantle's record of hitting safely in seven consecutive All-Star Games.

NL	4 0 1	0 0 0	0 2 0	—7
AL	0 0 0	0 0 2	1 0 2	—5

QUIZ 8

1. The Dodger pitcher who started the game, his fourth and last All-Star appearance, recorded his first win. Who was he?
2. Frankie Frisch, Lou Boudreau, and Willie Mays were the only men in All-Star history to accomplish this particular feat until Joe Morgan joined them in this game. What was that feat?
3. Joe Morgan and a Phillies outfielder became the tenth pair in All-Star history to hit two home runs in one inning. Who was that outfielder?
4. Who was the Dodger who hit the third home run for the NL?
5. Who set a new record for most assists by a second baseman in a nine-inning All-Star Game?
6. Who became the tenth pitcher in All-Star history to give up two home runs in one inning?
7. Who was the NL manager making his fourth and last appearance as an All-Star manager?
8. He was a coach in 1971 and 1975, but this was his first game as manager. Who was he?
9. Who was the game's MVP?
10. After a disastrous beginning, the last five AL pitchers settled

down to pitch a four-hitter over the last seven innings. How many can you name?

11. Who was the Red Sox player who hit the only home run for the AL?
12. Graig Nettles and Thurman Munson were struck out by a man who would be their teammate the next year. Who was he?

JULY 11, 1978, SAN DIEGO STADIUM, SAN DIEGO

National League 7/ American League 3

Attendance: 51,549

In spite of ten runs being scored on 18 hits, this was the first game in ten years and only the tenth game in All-Star history in which no home runs were hit.

The AL bolted to a 2–0 lead in the top of the first inning. The game was tied 3–3 after three innings, and it stayed that way until the bottom of the eighth, when the NL went ahead for good on a walk with the bases loaded. It was the seventh NL win in a row.

AL	2 0 1	0 0 0	0 0 0	— 3
NL	0 0 3	0 0 0	0 4 X	— 7

QUIZ 9

1. Who was the lead-off hitter for the AL who became the first player to hit two triples in one All-Star Game?
2. Who started for the NL, becoming the first pitcher in history to start an All-Star Game for each league?
3. Who was the AL pitcher who set a new All-Star record for allowing the most bases on balls in his career?
4. Who was the first repeat winner of the All-Star game's MVP award?
5. The losing pitcher went on to become the relief pitcher of the year, but he got shelled in the eighth inning to lose this game. Who was he?
6. Who scored on the AL's wild pitch in the bottom of the eighth?
7. Who was the AL catcher who allowed a passed ball?
8. Who was the Dodger manager who recorded his first All-Star win?

9. Who managed his second losing All-Star game in a row?
10. Who was the winning pitcher, a Cub making his first All-Star appearance?
11. Who did Jim Palmer walk in the third inning, with the bases loaded, to give the NL the go-ahead run?
12. Bob Boone (Phillies) and Ted Simmons (Cardinals) were two of the record-tying three catchers used by the NL in this game. Who was the third catcher?

JULY 17, 1979, KINGDOME, SEATTLE
National League 7/ American League 6
Attendance: 58,905

One of the most exciting games of the decade, the 1979 midsummer classic produced offensive and defensive thrills galore.

Lee Mazzilli hit the last All-Star home run of the decade, becoming the second pinch hitter to homer in his first All-Star trip to the plate. The only other man to do it was George Altman, in 1961. Reggie Jackson, Cookie Rojas, Willie Davis, and Carl Yastrzemski were the only other players in the 1970s to pinch-hit All-Star home runs.

It was not a pitcher's game. The NL used a record-tying seven pitchers as each team gave up ten hits. The 12 pitchers in the game struck out 10 batters but walked 11. Jim Kern joined only three others in All-Star history by committing a balk. Joaquin Andujar became the twenty-fourth All-Star pitcher to hit a batter, and he also threw a wild pitch. He does not match Juan Marichal's record of two wild pitches, in the ninth inning of the 1962 game.

The score was tied several times as the lead changed back and forth, and the final outcome was not settled until the final out of a thrilling ninth inning.

As the decade ended, the NL entered the record books by tying their previous mark of the most consecutive All-Star games (eight) won and, in fact, sweeping all but one of the ten games played in the 1970s.

NL	2 1 1	0 0 1	0 1 1	—7
AL	3 0 2	0 0 1	0 0 0	—6

QUIZ 10

1. The fans voted in an all–Red Sox outfield. Who were they?
2. Which one of them hit the only home run for the AL?
3. Twenty-seven players hold the record for coming to bat five times in one game. The two players who did it in this game were the top vote-getting outfielders for each league. Who were they?
4. Who was the NL outfielder who won the game's MVP with his arm, including one great throw that caught Brian Downing at the plate, when the score was tied?
5. The loss went to the only Texas Ranger on the roster. Who was he?
6. Jim Kern balked in this game, a miscue committed by only one other pitcher in the decade. Who was that Kansas City pitcher?
7. For the second time in the decade, the NL used seven pitchers. How many can you name?
8. Who was the AL left-hander who had the league's lowest ERA in 1979 but walked in the winning run in the ninth inning?
9. The losing manager appeared in four games himself, as a pitcher in the 1950s. Who was he?
10. The winning manager coached in the 1977 game and won the next two. Who was he?
11. The winning pitcher was a Cub relief ace who threw no-hit ball for the last two innings, striking out three, and winning his second straight All-Star game. Who was he?
12. Who were the only two NL All-Stars to receive over three million votes?

Quiz 1—Answers

1. Carl Yastrzemski, Red Sox, went 4 for 6 to join his predecessor, Ted Williams, who went 4 for 4 in 1946, and Ducky Medwick, who went 4 for 5 in 1937. Three of Yaz's hits were singles to tie him with six others: Charlie Gehringer, Billy Herman, Stan Hack, Bobby Avila, Ken Boyer, and Harmon Killebrew.
2. Dick Dietz, Giants, hit a homer in the bottom of the ninth in his only appearance in an All-Star game. He joined five others who had hit home runs in their first at-bat.
3. Tony Oliva's third double tied him with Al Simmons, Joe Cronin, Joe Gordon, Ted Kluszewski, and Ernie Banks.

4. Jim Palmer, Sam McDowell, Jim Perry, Catfish Hunter, Fritz Peterson, Mel Stottlemyre, and Clyde Wright.
5. Claude Osteen, Dodgers, pitched the last three innings, giving up three hits and no runs.
6. Clyde Wright pitched one and two-thirds innings, giving up three hits and one run.
7. Johnny Bench went 0 for 3 and joined nine others: Lou Gehrig, Bob Johnson, Stan Hack, Joe Gordon, Ken Keltner, Jim Hegan, Mickey Mantle, John Roseboro, and Willie McCovey. No player has struck out three times in one game since Bench.
8. The catcher was the Indians' Ray Fosse. It was Fosse's only appearance in an All-Star game, although he was still in the majors at the end of the decade.
9. Fritz Peterson, who was never on an All-Star squad again.
10. Jim Hickman hit a single with Pete Rose and Billy Grabarkewitz on base. It was his only All-Star appearance, and it came in the best season of his 13-year career. Hickman finished the year with the Cubs with 32 home runs, 102 runs, 115 RBIs, and a healthy .315 average.
11. Gil Hodges, whose Mets finished third in 1970 and 1971. He died in 1972 at the age of 48.
12. Earl Weaver, whose three Oriole pitchers, Jim Palmer, Mike Cuellar, and Dave McNally, went on to win 20, 24, and 24 games respectively in 1970.

Quiz 2—Answers

1. Reggie Jackson hit one over the second deck in right center. It was one of the longest home runs in All-Star history. Mickey Owen, Gus Bell, Larry Doby, Willie Mays, Stan Musial, Harmon Killebrew, George Altman, and Pete Runnels had pinch-hit home runs before him.
2. The AL had three (Frank Robinson, Reggie Jackson, and Harmon Killebrew); the NL had three (Hank Aaron, Johnny Bench, and Roberto Clemente). The only other games in which six home runs were hit were those of 1951 at Briggs Stadium and 1954 at Municipal Stadium.
3. Reggie Jackson and Frank Robinson (AL) hit their home runs

off Dock Ellis, and Hank Aaron (NL) hit his off Vida Blue. The record was set in 1951 and matched in 1954.

4. Luis Aparicio played in ten All-Star games and also holds the record for most putouts and total games by a shortstop. He had the amazing batting average of .071, 2 for 28. Juan Marichal pitched 18 innings in eight games, giving up only two runs on seven hits. He won two and lost none in All-Star competition. Jim Bunning and Don Drysdale also played in eight games.
5. Mort Cooper, Ed Lopat, Robin Roberts, Warren Spahn, John Wyatt, Milt Pappas, and Jim Maloney.
6. Earl Weaver used Jim Palmer and Mike Cuellar, both of whom went on to win 20 games in 1971.
7. Sparky Anderson played 152 games with the Phillies as a second baseman and hit .218. The previous year, 1970, was his first year as manager of Cincinnati.
8. Frank Robinson hit a home run off Early Wynn in 1959 when he was with Cincinnati.
9. Harmon Killebrew joined Bill White, who set the record when he was playing for the Cardinals.
10. Dock Ellis pitched three innings and gave up four runs on four hits.
11. Frank Robinson only went 1 for 2, but that was a home run with a man on base.
12. Mickey Lolich joined Johnny Vander Meer (1938) and Don Drysdale (1964.)

Quiz 3—Answers

1. Cookie Rojas who, interestingly, averaged fewer than four home runs a year over his 14-year career in the major leagues.
2. Hank Aaron. The greatest home-run hitter of all time hit only two home runs in 67 at-bats in All-Star games.
3. Tug McGraw, who struck out 92 men in 1972 and posted an ERA of 1.70 for the second season in a row.
4. Joc Morgan.
5. Dave McNally started the bottom of the tenth when the score was tied. He walked Nate Colbert and Chris Speier laid down a sacrifice bunt. When Joe Morgan singled, Colbert scored from second with the winning run.

6. Lee May had 13 putouts, compared to Harmon Killebrew's 15 in 1967.
7. Earl Weaver. This brought his record to one win and two losses.
8. Danny Murtaugh.
9. Rod Carew singled through the middle to give the AL a 1–0 lead.
10. Rod Carew and Cookie Rojas, who pinch-hit a two-run homer in the top of the eighth.
11. Aaron said that Gaylord Perry had served him up a spitter, but not one of his best spitters. Perry claimed, "Fastball, inside."
12. Carew had strained some muscles, so career understudy Rojas got his chance against Bill Stoneman.

Quiz 4—Answers

1. Willie Davis hit one for Don Sutton in the eighth.
2. Willie Mays had 75 at-bats, scored 20 runs, got 23 hits, 3 triples, and stole 6 bases. By comparison, Stan the Man had 63 at-bats, scored 11 runs, and had 20 hits.
3. The NL started Rick Wise (Cardinals), who pitched two innings and gave up one run. Dodgers Claude Osteen and Don Sutton followed; then Wayne Twitchell (Phillies), Dave Giusti (Pirates), Tom Seaver (Mets), and Jim Brewer (Dodgers). The AL started Catfish Hunter (A's), and teammate Ken Holtzman relieved in the second inning. Bert Blyleven (Twins), Bill Singer (Angels), Nolan Ryan (Angels), Sparky Lyle (Yankees), and Rollie Fingers (A's) followed.
4. Hank Aaron (Braves), Joe Torre (Cardinals), and Ron Fairly (Expos), went 1 for 5 among them, although they ended the year hitting .301, .287, and .298, respectively.
5. Brooks Robinson (Orioles) started, of course, followed by Sal Bando (A's) and Dave Nelson (Rangers). During the regular season, Nelson played 140 games at second base but none at third.
6. Joe Torre (Mets) and Ron Santo (Cubs).
7. Rick Wise started and gave up one run on two hits in two innings.

8. Bert Blyleven pitched one inning and gave up two runs on two hits.
9. Sparky Anderson.
10. Dick Williams, the Cincinnati manager.
11. The NL used Johnny Bench (Reds) and Ted Simmons (Cards). The AL used Carlton Fisk (Boston) and Thurman Munson (Yankees).
12. Amos Otis. Reggie Jackson (A's).

Quiz 5—Answers

1. Henry Aaron.
2. Brooks Robinson, the great third baseman for the Orioles, also set a record by playing in 18 games. The only players to come close are also "greats": Mickey Mantle (11 losses) and Stan Musial (10 losses).
3. It is Brooks Robinson again. "The human vacuum cleaner" made three double plays and tied the record set by Frank Malzone of the Red Sox, in seven games from 1957 through 1963.
4. Ken Brett entered the game in the fourth inning when the AL was ahead by one run. He pitched two innings and gave up one hit and no runs while walking one and striking out none. When he left the game, the NL had a lead, which they went on to build in later innings.
5. Luis Tiant went two innings and gave up three runs on four hits, while walking one and striking out none. In the two years in which he lost, 1968 and 1974, he went on to win 21 and 22 games, respectively, during the regular season.
6. Andy Messersmith, in his only All-Star appearance, gave up two runs on three bases on balls and two hits, while striking out four.
7. Johnny Bench and Thurman Munson, the great rivals, made one error each.
8. Yogi Berra. The first was, of course, Gil Hodges in 1970.
9. Dick Williams.
10. Gaylord Perry of the Cleveland Indians was with the Giants in 1970.
11. Reggie Smith.

12. Ron Cey. Mike Schmidt (Phillies) pinch-hit for him in the sixth, drawing a walk. He then replaced him at third.

Quiz 6—Answers

1. Jon Matlack pitched two innings and gave up no runs on two hits, while striking out Rod Carew, Bucky Dent, Gene Tenace, and Fred Lynn. Bill Madlock singled with the bases loaded in the ninth, scoring two runs and breaking the tie.
2. Carl Yastrzemski came up for Jim Kaat in the sixth inning and hit a three-run homer off Tom Seaver.
3. The player was Henry Aaron, and 24 All-Star games was the record. This game, his first as an ALer, was his last. He pinch-hit for Vida Blue and lined out.
4. Steve Garvey and Jim Wynn performed this feat off Vida Blue in the second inning. Al Rosen and Ray Boone did it in 1954, and Ted Williams and Mickey Mantle did it in 1956.
5. Claudell Washington, George Hendrick, and Graig Nettles joined the pilfering of Patrick Mullin, George McQuinn, and Mickey Vernon in 1948 and Willie Mays (twice) and Bill White in 1963.
6. The speedy Lou Brock went on to steal 56 bases that season, third in the league. The four men who set the record in 1934 were the AL's Charlie Gehringer and Heinie Manush and the NL's Mel Ott and Pie Traynor.
7. Reuss hit Thurman Munson with a pitch, and Gossage hit Larry Bowa. This was only the second game in which two batters were hit by pitches.
8. Joe Rudi.
9. Yogi Berra, who played in 15 All-Star games.
10. Catfish Hunter, whose previous loss was in 1967, when he was with Kansas City.
11. Mort Cooper (Cardinals), Claude Passeau (Cubs), Whitey Ford (Yankees), and Luis Tiant (Indians and Red Sox).
12. Henry Aaron hit two sacrifice flies in the 24 games in which he played. Clemente also hit two in 14 games.
13. Walt Alston, the manager of the Dodgers, also led the NL All-Stars to victory in 1956, 1960 (twice), 1964, 1966, and 1967.
14. Al Dark, manager of the Oakland A's.

Quiz 7—Answers

1. Randy Jones pitched three innings and gave up no runs on two hits, walking one and striking out one.
2. Mark Fidrych, "The Bird," pitched two innings and got tagged for two runs in the first inning.
3. Cesar Cedeno.
4. Rick Rhoden.
5. The starting center fielder, Fred Lynn.
6. Catfish Hunter.
7. Pete Rose (Reds), Ron Cey (Dodgers), and Mike Schmidt (Phillies).
8. It was not Al Kaline, who made his last All-Star appearance in 1974. It was Rusty Staub, who had appeared in three previous games as a National Leaguer.
9. The AL used Toby Harrah (Rangers), Mark Belanger (Orioles), and Fred Patek (Royals). The NL used Bill Russell (Dodgers), Dave Concepcion (Reds), and Larry Bowa (Phillies).
10. Sparky Anderson, whose All-Star teams won in 1971 and lost in 1973.
11. Darrell Johnson.
12. The Twins' Rod Carew, whose previous games were as a second baseman.

Quiz 8—Answers

1. It was Don Sutton.
2. The feat was hitting a home run as the lead-off batter at the start of a game.
3. Greg Luzinski.
4. Steve Garvey.
5. It was the Yankees' Willie Randolph, who had six assists.
6. Jim Palmer of the Orioles gave up the homers to Morgan and Luzinski in the top of the first inning. He also gave up the blast by Garvey, to become the first pitcher in All-Star history to allow three homers in one game.
7. Sparky Anderson.
8. Billy Martin.
9. Don Sutton gave up only one hit and no runs over the first three

innings, while striking out four (Randolph twice, Zisk, and Fisk).

10. Jim Kern (Indians), Dennis Eckersley (Indians), Dave LaRoche (Angels), Bill Campbell (Red Sox), and Sparky Lyle (Yankees).
11. George Scott.
12. The Pirates' Rich Gossage.

Quiz 9—Answers

1. It was the Twins' Rod Carew.
2. Vida Bluc of the Giants also started an All-Star game for the AL, when he was with the Oakland A's in 1971.
3. The Orioles' Jim Palmer added four walks in this game to the one each he gave up in the 1970, 1972, and 1977 games.
4. Steve Garvey, the winner in 1974, singled home two runs to tie the game in the third, and he tripled and scored the winning run in the eighth.
5. Rich Gossage gave up four runs on four hits. He struck out one, walked one, and threw a wild pitch.
6. Steve Garvey, who had just stroked an opposite-field triple.
7. The Rangers' Jim Sundberg.
8. Tom La Sorda.
9. It was the New York Yankees' #1, Billy Martin.
10. It was Bruce Sutter, who pitched to five batters and retired all of them, while striking out Jim Rice and Dwight Evans.
11. The Phillies' Greg Luzinski.
12. It was not Johnny Bench, but rather the man who replaced him because of injury. The Braves' Biff Pocoroba played but did not get to bat.

Quiz 10—Answers

1. Jim Rice, Fred Lynn, and Carl Yastrzemski. They went 4 for 9, with three RBIs among them.
2. Fred Lynn hit one with one on, off the Phillies' Steve Carlton.
3. The Padres' Dave Winfield and the Red Sox's Jim Rice.
4. The Pirates' Dave Parker made two sensational throws from right field.
5. Jim Kern pitched two and two-thirds innings and gave up two

runs. He left the game in the top of the ninth, with two outs and the bases loaded.

6. Steve Busby balked in the 1975 game.
7. Steve Carlton (Phillies), Joaquin Andujar (Astros), Steve Rogers (Expos), Gaylord Perry (Padres), Joe Sambito (Astros), Mike La Coss (Reds), and Bruce Sutter (Cubs).
8. Ron Guidry (Yankees) was brought in with two outs and the bases loaded. He walked the Mets' Lee Mazzilli.
9. Bob Lemon pitched six and two-thirds All-Star innings when he was with the Indians, registering no wins and one loss. He was not managing at the time the All-Star game was played, having been fired early in the 1979 season.
10. Tom La Sorda, the Dodgers' manager.
11. Bruce Sutter.
12. Mike Schmidt (Phillies) and Dave Winfield (Padres).

CHAMPIONSHIP SERIES AND WORLD SERIES

The first modern World Series was held in 1903 between Pittsburgh and Boston. Pittsburgh, under Manager Fred Clarke, had breezed to a big lead over John McGraw's Giants, and Jimmy Collins' Boston club had posted an almost identical mark while walking away with the AL pennant ahead of Connie Mack's Philadelphia team.

The best of nine series was arranged by the presidents of the two teams who agreed to divide the receipts equally between them, making their own arrangements with the players.

The series began on October 1, which complicated matters because the contracts of the Boston players expired on September 30 while those of the Pittsburgh players ran until October 15. The series went eight games, drawing a total crowd of 100,430 and netting approximately $50,000. The ensuing squabble over payments to players ended up in confusion as the losing club got more money per player than the winner.

Boston boasted three 20-game winners: Cy Young who had a 28–9 record, Bill Dineen who had a 21–12 record, and Long Tom Hughes who had a 20–7 record. Patsy Dougherty and Buck Freeman were among the league leaders in virtually all offensive categories, including Freeman's 13 home runs.

Deacon Phillippe and Sam Leever had won 50 games for Pittsburgh between them but they had lost the great Jack Chesbro to New York in the American League the year before. Honus Wagner,

Ginger Beaumont, and Fred Clark provided the offensive firepower, featuring Wagner's .355 batting average.

The first three games were played in Boston and after the fourth in Pittsburgh, Boston was down three games to one, setting the stage for one of the great comebacks in baseball history.

The story of Boston's sweep of the next four games can be stated briefly. In two words, the Boston comeback was Young and Dineen. Each won two games and each pitcher had two complete games. In the last four games, these two iron men gave up a total of 8 runs on 30 hits.

The biggest heroes were Dineen, who won three games; Young, who won two; and Dougherty, who hit two home runs and had five RBIs. The only man Boston called in relief was Cy Young, who went seven innings in game two. Both teams used a total of only eight pitchers in the eight games, Boston using only three pitchers: Young, Dineen, and Hughes. This series still stands in the record books as the one in which the fewest number of pitchers were used by both clubs and by one club. By contrast, Cincinnati and Boston used a total of twelve pitchers in just one game, their extra-inning contest in the sixth game of the 1975 World Series.

Pittsburgh's mighty Honus Wagner bore the brunt of the loss. The Flying Dutchman hit only .222 and made three of his team's ten errors. Outfielder Jimmy Sebring batted .367 and hit Pittsburgh's lone home run, the first ever hit in World Series play.

The two leagues could not reconcile their differences in 1904 but they came to terms in 1905 and the World Series has continued without interruption since then. The attendance at two World Series games is now well in excess of the number of people who attended all of the first eight games. In addition, over 60 million people now watch the World Series on television.

In 1903, there were only eight teams in each league. By 1968 the number had grown to twenty and the smell of continued expansion was in the air. By the end of the 1970s, there were twelve teams in the National League and fourteen teams in the American League. The Championship Series was added in 1968 as a measure to increase regional competition and to add one more thrill, the penultimate one, in order to decide the two teams, one from each league, that would meet in the October Classic, the World Series.

1970 CHAMPIONSHIP SERIES

American League

	W	L
Baltimore (East)	3	0
Minnesota (West)	0	3

National League

	W	L
Cincinnati (West)	3	0
Pittsburgh (East)	0	3

In the AL, Baltimore beat Minnesota, three games to none, as they had done the year before. For the Orioles, this meant six straight wins in champtionship play, and for the Twins it meant six straight losses.

Baltimore had both the hitting and the pitching. They outhit Minnesota 36 hits to 24, and they belted six home runs to the Twins' three. One of the Oriole round-trippers was a grand slam pop in the opener by Mike Cuellar, a pitcher with a lifetime batting average slightly over .100.

Dick Hall came in to save the opening game, as he had the year before, and both Jim Palmer and Dave McNally turned in complete games. Palmer struck out 12 men while winning the third game.

It was not the mighty bats of the Cincinnati Reds that won the NL series for them, but rather it was their pitching staff, which was considered to be very questionable because of injuries. Pete Rose, Johnny Bench, Tony Perez, and company produced only nine runs over the three games but seven pitchers from the Reds' staff collaborated for an incredible .96 ERA as they held the powerful Pirates to only 23 hits and three runs over 28 innings. Gary Nolan pitched nine innings of shutout ball in the opener, and Clay Carroll and Don Gullett got two saves each.

The scene was set for Earl Weaver's Orioles to meet Sparky Anderson's Big Red Machine, as Baltimore would try to atone for their humiliating upset by the Mets in the 1969 World Series.

1970 WORLD SERIES

	W	L
Baltimore (AL)	4	1
Cincinnati (NL)	1	4

The opening game on October 10 was the first World Series game to be played at Cincinnati's Riverfront Stadium, and it was the first to be played on artificial turf.

In spite of excellent performances by Clay Carroll and Don Gullett in relief, the Redleg pitching staff, weakened as well as depleted by injuries, fell apart before the hitting onslaught of the Orioles. Baltimore's 32 RBIs set a new record for a five-game series, as did their ten home runs. The Robinsons, Brooks, and Frank, hit two homers each, and Boog Powell hit two more.

One of the memorable incidents of this series was the very controversial call at home plate in the first game. Ellie Hendricks, the Oriole catcher, picked up a hit ball in front of the plate. Jim Palmer called to him to tag Bernie Carbo, who was racing home from third. Hendricks spun around and, as he leaped to tag Carbo, he collided with umpire Ken Burkhart, who was straddling the third-base line. From the mass confusion of bodies at the plate came the umpire's out signal, and from the Cincinnati dugout came Sparky Anderson. The fans at home were treated to replay after replay and stop-action photos clearly showing that Hendricks had tagged Carbo with his gloved left hand while holding the ball in his right hand. To add fat to the fire, Carbo didn't touch the plate.

Another thing about this series that fans will long remember is the almost unparalleled play of Brooks Robinson, who led his Baltimore team with both glove and bat. He made one impossible fielding play after another, hit .429, and had six RBIs.

The goat of the series was the unfortunate Tony Perez. He had a fantastic year in 1970, hitting .317, with 40 home runs and 129 RBIs during the regular season. In 18 trips to the plate in this Series, he could not muster more than one single, for an .056 batting average. It was an unfortunate end to a dream for Tony Perez and his Big Red Machine.

1970 QUIZ

1. Who was the batter, a pinch hitter, who hit the chop in front of the plate that caused all the controversy in the Hendricks–Carbo play at home?
2. Who was the first pitcher ever to hit a grand-slam home run in a World Series as well as the only pitcher besides Bob Gibson to hit a home run in two different World Series games?
3. Mike Cuellar, Jim Palmer, and Dave McNally got three of Baltimore's wins. Who got the fourth?

4. Who was the Baltimore outfielder who tied the World Series record by hitting eight singles in a five-game Series?
5. Who was the Cincinnati infielder who tied a 60-year-old record by knocking in eight runs in a five-game Series?
6. Who were the two Orioles who tied the record of nine hits in a five-game Series?
7. Who was the Cincinnati player who set the record of starting the most double plays in a five-game Series?
8. Who were the two first basemen—one with Cincinnati, one with Baltimore—who scored six runs each in this five-game Series, tying a record last held by Al Simmons in 1929?
9. Who was the Baltimore infielder who became the thirty-third man in World Series history to get four hits in one game?
10. Who was the Baltimore player who had a higher batting average for the Series than Brooks Robinson?

1971 CHAMPIONSHIP SERIES

American League	W	L	*National League*	W	L
Baltimore (East)	3	0	Pittsburgh (East)	3	1
Oakland (West)	0	3	San Francisco (West)	1	3

Baltimore and Oakland each ran away with their division, finishing in first place 12 and 16 games ahead of the nearest competitor. It was the third year in a row that Baltimore had won over 100 games and won its division. As for the Oakland A's, formerly the Kansas City Athletics and, before that, the Philadelphia Athletics, Dick Williams took them to first place with 101 wins, and it was the first time the A's had won more than 100 games since 1931.

Baltimore finished the season with the most awesome pitching staff in 50 years; it was even better than Cleveland's combination of Early Wynn, Bob Lemon, Mike Garcia, and Bob Feller of the early 1950s. Mike Cuellar, Pat Dobson, Jim Palmer, and Dave McNally had compiled an 81–31 record in 1971, and baseball had not seen four 20-game winners on the same team since 1920. That year, the Chicago White Sox finished second to Tris Speaker's Indians, in spite of the 87–44 record posted by Eddie Cicotte, Red Faber, Dickie Kerr, and Lefty Williams.

Oakland had a good pitching staff in Vida Blue and Catfish Hunter, both 20-game winners, and they were supplemented by Chris Dobson, Diego Segui, and Blue Moon Odom. With Rollie Fingers and Darold Knowles in the bullpen, the A's clearly had better relief pitching. Knowledgeable fans looked for a long playoff in the American League, one filled with pitchers' duels.

Baltimore blew away the A's in three straight. Cuellar and Palmer pitched complete games, Palmer's third in a row in championship series, and McNally pitched seven strong innings before leaving for Eddie Watt, who got the save. Seven home runs were hit, two each by Boog Powell and Reggie Jackson.

Danny Murtaugh took his Pittsburgh Pirates to their second division championship in two years, and, in the NL West, Charlie Fox's San Francisco Giants just edged out the Dodgers. The encounter took shape as one between the bats of Willie Stargell, Roberto Clemente, Dave Cash, and Manny Sanguillen and the pitching of Gaylord Perry.

The bats won. Yet it was not Stargell, who went 0 for 14, but young Bob Robertson who led the Pirates, with a .438 batting average, six RBIs, and four home runs, three of them consecutive.

Gaylord Perry pitched a complete game in the opener, but Pittsburgh came back to win the next three in a row. Marichal went all the way in the third game but lost a four-hitter by a 2–1 score. Perry went to the mound again in game four and tried to even up the series, but he was rocked by seven runs in five and two-thirds innings.

The scene was ready to shift to Baltimore's Memorial Stadium, where the Orioles would try to defend their World Championship against the Pittsburgh Pirates, seeing their first World Series victory since a stroke of Bill Mazeroski's bat had given them the win over the New York Yankees in the bottom of the ninth in game seven in 1960.

Everyone knows that good pitching has it all over good hitting in a brief series, and that is one of the reasons why Baltimore was installed as a 9–5 favorite to win the Series. My money was on Baltimore.

1971 WORLD SERIES

	W	L
Pittsburgh (NL)	4	3
Baltimore (AL)	3	4

After Dave McNally and Jim Palmer had coasted to 5–3 and 11–3 wins in the first two games of the Series, the wise old heads that had predicted a Baltimore romp began to nod in anticipation.

The Orioles could have come close to winning the third game in a row, had Bob Robertson not missed a signal at the plate. With Roberto Clemente and Willie Stargell on base in the seventh inning with no outs, and with Pittsburgh nursing a slim 2–1 lead, conventional wisdom called for a sacrifice bunt to move the runners ahead. In spite of the fact that Robertson had hit three home runs in a row in one game in the playoffs, he was given the signal to bunt. He missed the signal and blasted a three-run homer into the right-field seats.

Robertson had hit 26 home runs during the 1971 season and 27 the year before. Jim Murray wrote in the *Los Angeles Times* that the reason he missed the signal to bunt was that he had never seen one before. He had not bunted all season.

In any event, Robertson's three insurance runs proved to be more than Steve Blass needed, as he went the route with a three-hitter, giving up just one run.

The fourth game, at Three Rivers Stadium in Pittsburgh, was the first night game in history, and the stadium was filled to capacity. A national TV audience of more than 60 million added to the drama.

Pittsburgh starter Luke Walker was knocked out of the box in the first inning and, behind by three runs, Danny Murtaugh called rookie Bruce Kison out of the bullpen. Kison, less than a week away from his wedding, had faced two batters in game two and walked both of them. However, he was up to the moment this time, and he allowed only one hit until Dave Giusti relieved him in the eighth.

The unlikely hero of game number five was Nelson Briles. He had been traded from the Cardinals after a 6–7 season with a 6.22 ERA in 1970. With an 8–4 record, he appeared to be mismatched against Dave McNally, the winner of the opening game. Briles went all the way, pitching a two-hitter and knocking in a run.

After nine innings of game six, the score was 2–2, as Palmer sprinkled eight hits over nine innings. In the tenth inning, Brooks Robinson hit a short sacrifice fly and scored Frank Robinson, who slid between Sanguillen's legs with the game-winning run.

The last game was a marvelous pitching duel, with Steve Blass again going all the way and giving up only four hits in nine innings. Cuellar, Dobson, and McNally gave up only six hits. With their 2–1 victory, the Pirates became the first team to come back from losing the first two games to win a World Championship.

Roberto Clemente was 12 for 29, hitting safely in all seven games, and batting .414. He walked twice, hit two doubles, a triple, and two home runs, scored three, and knocked in four. Clemente got the recognition he so deserved, but, in many people's minds, the real heroes of the 1971 World Series were the members of the much maligned, no-name pitching staff of the Pittsburgh Pirates: a youngster named Bruce Kison, a pitcher considered to be over the hill by the name of Nellie Briles, and, most of all, the unheralded right-hander from Canaan, Connecticut, by the name of Steve Blass. Blass pitched two complete games and won both, while striking out 13 and giving up only seven hits. He had an ERA of 1.00 over 18 innings.

So much for conventional wisdom.

1971 QUIZ

1. In the eighth inning of the last game, who raced from first to home on a double?
2. Who hit that game-winning double?
3. Who tied a World Series record by appearing in five games as a pinch hitter?
4. Who was the Oriole who tied the record held by seven players by playing three different positions in one Series?
5. Which team—Pittsburgh or Baltimore—had the lowest ERA for the Series?
6. What was the controversy regarding Pat Dobson about?
7. When this player reached first base safely five times while hitting 1.000 in a nine-inning game, he joined Babe Ruth (twice)

and Lou Brock as only the third player in World Series history to do so. Who was the Oriole who did this?

8. Who was the Oriole who brought his World Series total of being hit by a pitch to a record-tying three? He had been hit twice before, in the 1961 Series.
9. Only 15 players in World Series history had gotten two hits in one inning before this Baltimore outfielder added his name to the record books. Who was he?
10. Why was Earl Weaver criticized over his use of Boog Powell in the Series?

1972 CHAMPIONSHIP SERIES

American League

	W	L
Oakland (West)	3	2
Detroit (East)	2	3

National League

	W	L
Cincinnati (West)	3	2
Pittsburgh (East)	2	3

Billy Martin's Detroit Tigers just edged out the Boston Red Sox in the East, while Dick Williams's Oakland A's coasted to their second straight win in the West.

Each team sent its pitching ace to the mound in the first game. Mickey Lolich dueled Catfish Hunter throughout the game, and it went into the eleventh inning as a 1–1 tie. Al Kaline went from hero to goat as he homered in the top of the elventh but made a throwing error in the bottom of the inning, allowing the winning run to score.

Blue Moon Odom pitched a three-hitter, a complete game, and walked none to bring the Oakland edge to two games to one. The second game will be long remembered as containing one of the more unfortunate incidents in baseball history.

When Bert Campaneris led off the seventh inning, he had already singled three times, stolen second and third, and scored twice. Young Lerrin LaGrow, who had appeared in only 16 games all season, hit Campaneris on the ankle with his first pitch. Campaneris, outmatched by seven inches and 60 pounds, wound up and threw his bat at LaGrow. Both benches emptied, with Billy Martin leading the Tigers from the dugout. Both players were ejected from the game, and Campaneris was suspended for the rest of the playoffs. In a very questionable decision, AL president Joe Cronin let Campaneris play in the World Series but also suspended him from the first seven games of the 1973 season.

In the third game, Detroit's Joe Coleman set a new playoff record by fanning 14 while scattering seven hits and pitching a shutout. As the Tigers came to bat in the bottom of the tenth inning of the fourth game, they were down 3–1 and it looked hopeless. However, Detroit put together two singles, a wild pitch, a walk, and an error to produce one run. Anoter walk, with the bases loaded, and a single, drew the series all even at two apiece.

Blue Moon Odom, with Vida Blue in relief, gave Oakland its first American League pennant in 42 years. Not since Connie Mack had taken the Athletics to their third pennant in a row in 1931 had the team been in the World Series.

Steve Blass, hero of the 1971 World Series, won the opener for Pittsburgh. Starter Bob Moose gave up five hits in a row without retiring a batter before being taken out of the second game, which Cincinnati went on to win.

Manny Sanguillen hit a homer for one run and knocked in the winning run in the third game behind the strong pitching of Briles, Kison, and Giusti. Ross Grimsley evened up the series with a two-hitter, while pitching a complete game for Cincinnati in the fourth game.

After a rain delay of an hour and a half, the climactic fifth game began. The Reds were behind 3–2 as they came to bat in the bottom of the ninth, only three outs away from defeat. After Dave Giusti gave up a home run to Johnny Bench and singles to Tony Perez and Denis Menke, Bill Virdon called Bob Moose in from the bullpen. Moose had started 30 games in 1972 and had a 13–10 record, but he had pitched only once in relief. After getting Cesar Geronimo to fly out and making Darrel Chaney pop up, disaster struck. Moose bounced a wild pitch into the dirt, and pinch runner George Foster raced home with the winning run, which put the Reds into the World Series for the second time in the 1970s.

As Joe Durso noted in *The New York Times*, "It was a chaotic finish to a playoff that went the five-game limit, with the Pirates leading all the way in the defense of their world title—until the last inning."

1972 WORLD SERIES

	W	L
Oakland (AL)	4	3
Cincinnati (NL)	3	4

The ever-increasing importance of television to baseball became evident when a new schedule was unveiled, starting with this Series. The first two games were played on Saturday and Sunday afternoons, followed by a day off and three night games. After another day off, the last two games were also to be day games on Saturday and Sunday.

The two teams seemed as evenly matched as possible. Oakland had won 101 games, and Cincinnati had won 95. The two pitching staffs had only one 20-game winner—Catfish Hunter—between them. Oakland's bullpen boasted Rollie Fingers, Bob Locker, and Darold Knowles, who had amassed 42 saves among them: Cincinnati's Clay Carroll had led the National League with 37 saves, and Pedro Borbon had 11.

The regular lineups showed one .300 hitter for each team: Pete Rose and Joe Rudi. What the Cincinnati Reds decidedly did have was the MVP of the year in Johnny Bench, who had led the league with 40 home runs and 125 RBIs. What the Oakland A's did not have was Reggie Jackson, who had hit 26 home runs, with 75 RBIs. Since Mr. October had pulled a hamstring and would not be available for any service in the World Series, the judicious handicapper gave the edge to Cincinnati. There apparently was not anyone on the bench who could take up the slack caused by Reggie's absence.

The man of the hour whom the A's needed so desperately emerged in the person of Gene Tenace. Some National League fans had to be told that his last name was pronounced like the little ball people hit back and forth over a net. After starting in the minors in 1965, Tenace spent his first full season with Oakland in 1971. In 1972, he had caught only 49 games, while also being used in the outfield and at first, second, and third. The regular catcher, Dave Duncan, spent most of the Series on the bench, with only three at-bats, and he was traded to Cleveland the next year. Gene Tenace spent the Series carving his name into the record book.

He knocked in all three Oakland runs in their winning effort in the first game; he accounted for nine of his team's RBIs; he hit .348; he tied a World Series record by hitting four home runs.

Joe Rudi hit a home run in the second game, and he also made a spectacular game-saving catch of a Denis Menke line drive. Hunter got the win for the A's, and Fingers came in for the final out.

In the third game, Blue Moon Odom struck out 11, and he, Blue, and Fingers only gave up four hits, but they lost a heartbreaker as Billingham and Carroll gave up three hits and combined for a shutout for Cincinnati's first win.

Oakland won the fourth game as Tenace hit a home run, but they lost the fifth in spite of another homer by Tenace, this one with two men on base. Cincinnati won the fifth game, with a great deal of thanks to the speed of Joe Morgan. He scored one run by coming home from first on a hit-and-run play with Bobby Tolan at the plate. He later walked, stole second, and scored again on a single by Tolan. The sixth game was a romp for the Reds, as they rocked the Oakland pitchers for eight runs on ten hits.

The final game was tied at one apiece when Tenace doubled home Bert Campaneris for what was to prove to be the winning run. The pinch runner for Tenace also scored when Tolan pulled a hamstring racing after a Sal Bando line drive. The Reds came back with one more run in the eighth, but that was the end of their scoring. They came up two runs short of winning the final game and the World Championship.

It was as close a series as everyone had figured. Both teams had identical batting averages of .209, 46 hits in 220 at-bats. Rudi, Rose, and Bench came through with home runs, and Cincinnati kept it interesting with the speed of Morgan and Tolan. Only one of the seven games was decided by more than one run. When the scores for the seven games were added up, the losers had scored five more runs than the winners. That meant, of course, that the losing pitching staff had a better ERA than the winning pitching staff.

Catfish Hunter got his win; as a matter of fact, he had two wins for Oakland, but Cincinnati's Ross Grimsley also won two. Fingers and Blue had three saves, but so did Carroll, Billingham, and Hall.

In the final analysis, the difference between these two excellent clubs was a brand-new star, whom his parents had aptly named

Fury but who is better known to us as Gene Tenace. The baseball world now knew how to pronounce his name.

1972 QUIZ

1. Who was the Oakland player who set a new World Series record by being used as a pinch runner in six games?
2. Who was the Oakland catcher who became only the twelfth player in World Series history to hit back-to-back home runs in the same game?
3. Who was the big right-hander who came to Cincinnati as part of the big package trade with Houston that included Joe Morgan, Denis Menke, Cesar Geronimo, and Ed Armbrister? He pitched 13⅔ innings of hitless ball in three games in the Series, while striking out 11.
4. Who was the Cincinnati first baseman who was such a disappointment at the plate in the 1970 World Series, but who led his team with a .435 batting average in this Series?
5. Who was the Oakland player who got three pinch hits, tying the record held by Bobby Brown (1947), Dusty Rhodes (1954), and Carl Warwick (1964)?
6. Who was the Cincinnati outfielder who became only the eleventh player to lead off a World Series game with a home run?
7. Who was the pitcher who tied the record held by three players, by winning two games and losing none in relief?
8. The fifth inning of the third game was the first time in World Series history that both pitchers struck out the side in the same inning. Who were the two pitchers?
9. Who had the highest slugging average in a seven-game Series of any player in history?
10. Oakland sent three pinch hitters to the plate in the ninth inning of game four, and they responded by setting a new World Series record by getting three singles. Who were those three pinch hitters?

1973 CHAMPIONSHIP SERIES

American League	W	L	*National League*	W	L
Oakland (West)	3	2	New York (East)	3	2
Baltimore (East)	2	3	Cincinnati (West)	2	3

In the American League, the cast for the 1973 championship series was the same as it had been in 1971. For the third time in the 1970s, Earl Weaver's Baltimore Orioles captured first place in the East with a handy eight-game lead over the Boston Red Sox. Dick Williams's Oakland A's won the Western Division, six games over Kansas City. For Oakland, this was the third straight year in which they had finished first in their division, but they were facing a team that had never lost a playoff game.

The Orioles' pitching staff looked weaker than when they had last faced Oakland; they certainly did not have as impressive a record, and Pat Dobson had been traded to Atlanta. Oakland's staff looked better, now boasting three 20-game winners. The bats of Reggie Jackson and Sal Bando did not seem to be matched by the power Baltimore had shown. Charlie Finley's budding dynasty could sweep this series.

Jim Palmer, one of the great pitchers when the chips are down, shut out Oakland in the opener, on a five-hitter. The second game was more like what the fans were expecting, as Oakland won on the pitching of Catfish Hunter and four A's home runs. The third game pitted Mike Cuellar and Ken Holtzman against each other until the eleventh inning, when the game was settled in Oakland's favor on a Campaneris home run. Baltimore came back in the fifth game, but Hunter finished them off in the sixth game, with a brilliant shutout, a five-hitter.

After spending two months in last place, the Mets made one of the great comebacks of all time when they finally nailed down first place in the NL East by beating the Cubs one day after the season was supposed to have ended. Yogi Berra had won the honor of throwing his pitching staff against the mighty bats of the Cincinnati Reds, who had edged out the Dodgers in the West.

A sore-armed Tom Seaver struck out 13 Reds in the opener, but he lost the 2–1 game on home runs by Rose and Bench. Jon Matlack threw a two-hitter in the second game to even up the series, and the action moved to New York.

"Action" is an understatement to describe the disgraceful events of that October 8 game at Shea Stadium. In the second inning, Pete Rose slid into Bud Harrelson at second as he was attempting to break up a double play. Rose slid the only way he knows how—hard. The feisty Harrelson, all 150 pounds of him, took exception, and a fight ensued. Like most baseball fights, this one was more light than heat, and order was shortly restored on the field.

Order was not restored in the stands, however, The Mets fans, never known for their restraint, threw beer cans and miscellaneous garbage at Rose when he took his place in left field. When a whiskey bottle narrowly missed Rose, Sparky Anderson quickly and wisely pulled his team off the field. NL president Chub Feeney asked Yogi Berra and Willie Mays, two of New York's most beloved ballplayers, to talk to the fans in an attempt to restore peace and order. Tom Seaver, Rusty Staub, and Cleon Jones joined them, and the world was greeted by the sight of Willie Mays, one of the greatest players in history, having to stretch his arms out to his own fans and beg them to stop acting like drunken hooligans.

Many writers have compared this black moment to the Ducky Medwick incident in the 1934 World Series, but there were two significant differences. When Medwick was pelted with debris in left field at Tiger Stadium in Detroit, Commissioner Landis ordered him removed so that the game could continue. Medwick's team, the St. Louis Cardinals, were ahead 11–0 in the seventh inning. At Shea Stadium, the Mets were ahead 5–2, and they would have forfeited the game had some kind of order not been imposed. Another difference is that Ducky Medwick slid into Marvin Owen, the Tiger third baseman, with spikes high, and Owen was cut by the play. Rose slid in with hands, not spikes, high. Although he admitted that he wanted to knock Harrelson into left field, Rose never played dirty, just hard. Players can accept this, but too many fans cannot.

The Reds won the fifth game on one home run by Perez and another by Rose, the latter coming in the twelfth inning. The final act of what was becoming an ugly play would be at Shea Stadium with the protagonists of the opener—Jack Billingham and Tom Seaver—again facing each other. Seaver and McGraw combined for a 7–2 win, repeating the miracle of 1969. Pandemonium again erupted.

But it was different. As Leonard Koppett reported in his history of the New York Mets, "Unlike the wild scenes of 1969, this . . . had an undercurrent of viciousness and random destructiveness. The Reds thought Rose might be attacked, and formed a protective cordon. Some players' wives, along with uncounted innocents, were all but trampled in the stands and seriously frightened!"

We must remember that it was the so-called fans, not the players, who gave this series its bad name. The games on the field were brilliant baseball, baseball at its best.

1973 WORLD SERIES

	W	L
Oakland (AL)	4	3
New York (NL)	3	4

The 1973 World Series promised to be everything a fan could ask for. It was to be a confrontation between a team owned by the loveable Joan Shipman Payson and one owned by the controversial, cantankerous Charlie Finley; it would be the remnants of a team built by Casey Stengel and glued together by Yogi Berra against a new American League dynasty in the making; it would be the classic matchup of pitching versus hitting, a boxer versus a slugger; it would be East against West; it would be the New York Mets against the Oakland A's.

As Sy Burick of *The Dayton Daily News* noted in his analysis of the opening game, you would have to be a hardhearted villain not to cry a little for Felix Millan, the Mets' second baseman who was the goat of the opener. The A's scored two runs after Millan let a routine ground ball through his legs.

The second game saw more tears shed, these for Willie Mays. The 42-year-old superstar fell on his face in center field chasing what would have been for him, in the past, a routine line drive. After almost 11,000 at-bats, this Series would be the farewell performance for the Say-Hey Kid from Alabama.

Game number two will be indelibly etched in the memories of those who saw it. It was the longest game in World Series history, taking 4 hours and 13 minutes. Twenty-seven runners were left on base, a new record, and the total of 11 pitchers tied a record. The six errors did not set a new record, but they came close, and two of those errors caused the big controversy of the Series.

In the top of the twelfth inning, Mike Andrews, who had played only 18 games with the A's after starting the year with the White Sox, let a routine grounder go through his legs, scoring two runs. Another run scored on the next play when Andrews threw wide to first, drawing Tenace off the bag. The A's went on to win 10–7.

Andrews did set a new World Series record for a second baseman by making two errors in one inning. This is not something to laugh about, but it is hardly the end of the world. Hank Greenberg, Roger Peckinpaugh, Frank Torre, and Pee Wee Reese are a few of the other players who committed two errors in one inning in World Series play.

When Millan cost the Mets the first game with an error, Yogi Berra showed his class by saying, "I just hope they hit every ball to him."

The day after Andrews committed two errors, Charlie Finley showed *his* class by "firing" Andrews and sending him home in disgrace. Commissioner Bowie Kuhn ordered Finley to reinstate him immediately, and the Oakland players found themselves in the middle of another Finley fracas.

Oakland won game three, but the Mets fought back to win the next two, scratching out 2–0 and 3–1 wins behind the pitching of Jerry Koosman and Tom Seaver, with McGraw in relief in both games.

Oakland squeaked out a win in the eleventh inning of the third game in spite of Tom Seaver's valiant effort; 12 strikeouts in eight innings. Rusty Staub provided all the runs needed for Jon Matlack, who pitched a three-hitter, as the Mets won the fourth game and evened up the Series. New York and Oakland alternated wins in the next two outings, providing for a seventh game, the showdown in California.

The pitchers of the opening game, Matlack and Holtzman, faced each other once again. It might have suddenly dawned on the A's that they had not yet hit a home run. Jackson and Campaneris remedied that situation in the third inning, when they each hit two-run shots, providing Oakland with all the runs they needed. Their 5–2 win in the seventh game gave them their second straight World Championship. They became the first team to win consecutive World Series since the New York Yankees beat Cincinnati and San Francisco in 1961 and 1962.

The great East-West shootout had lived up to its advance billing. Oakland and New York had tied or set new records for: most pinch-hitters used in a series, both clubs (34); fewest complete games (none); most left on base, both clubs (130); and, of course, the myriad of records set in the second game, the longest in World Series history.

Dave Anderson of *The New York Times* reported that Bud Harrelson looked up from the solemn quiet of the Mets locker room after the Series and spoke. "Anybody want to buy some unused bats?" He was referring to a new shipment of bats that had just arrived, but he could just as well have been referring to the record-setting number of 72 Mets left on base.

Reggie Jackson, so often the center of turmoil, tried to forget the bad parts of the season, including an invidious death threat against him in the Series. A year before, the epitome of despair, he had watched the World Series on crutches, but this year he was more than happy with his .310 batting average, having knocked in 6 of his team's 20 runs. He hit two doubles to win game six and a home run to win game seven.

Then, as now, Reggie did not want to talk about his manager or the owner of his club. He told newspaper reporters after the Series that all he wanted to do was hit and run and jump and throw and slide and get dirty. Don't we all?

1973 QUIZ

1. Who was the Met who had played in his first World Series 22 years earlier?
2. Who was the catcher who tied a record he would rather forget by having 30 at-bats without a hit?
3. Who was the Oakland player who tied Babe Ruth's record (1926) by getting 11 bases on balls in one Series?
4. Who was the Met who became the fifth player to get three pinch-hits in one World Series?

5. Who was the Mets' third baseman who tied Eddie Matthews's 1958 record by striking out 11 times in one Series?
6. Who tied a World Series record by appearing in five games as a pinch hitter?
7. Who were the two outfielders—one the Oakland center fielder, the other the Met right fielder—to become the thirty-fourth and thirty-fifth players in history to get four hits in one game?
8. Who was the Mets' second baseman who had the dubious distinction of becoming only the third man in World Series history to go 0 for 6 in an extra-inning game?
9. Who was the Mets outfielder who reached first base safely five times while hitting 1.000, to become only the fourth man in World Series history to do so?
10. Who was the relief pitcher who set a new record by appearing in seven games?

1974 CHAMPIONSHIP SERIES

American League	W	L	*National League*	W	L
Oakland (West)	3	1	Los Angeles (West)	3	1
Baltimore (East)	1	3	Pittsburgh (East)	1	3

Dick Williams had quit the A's after the 1973 World Series, as much in disgust as anything else. He reemerged in 1974 as the manager of the California Angels. With a new skipper, Alvin Dark, at the helm, Oakland breezed to a first-place finish for the fourth year in a row. Dark, who had managed the San Francisco Giants in their 1962 loss to the Yankees, became only the third manager to win pennants in both leagues. Yogi Berra won with the Yankees in 1964 and the Mets in 1973, and Joe McCarthy won with the Cubs in 1929 and with the Yankees eight times in the 1930s and 1940s.

For the fifth time in the six years since the playoffs were initiated, Earl Weaver's Orioles took first place in the AL East.

Baltimore beat up on 25-game winner Catfish Hunter in the opener, tagging him for three home runs in less than five innings. Cuellar got the win for the Orioles, with Ross Grimsley in relief.

The next three games followed, more or less, the script that experts had written for the 1973 playoffs and dusted off again for this one. Truly outstanding efforts by McNally, Palmer, Cuellar, and the Baltimore reliefers fell just short of even more outstanding performances by Holtzman, Blue, Hunter, and Fingers. Oakland swept the second, third, and fourth games 5–0, 1–0, and 2–1, as their pitching staff allowed just 12 hits in three games. The bats of Ray Fosse, Sal Bando, and Reggie Jackson provided all the offense that was needed.

In the NL, Walt Alston's Los Angeles Dodgers held off a late-season surge by the Cincinnati Reds to win the Western Division. Danny Murtaugh's Pittsburgh Pirates edged out the St. Louis Cardinals on the last day of the season. It was the fourth time in the 1970s that they had won the NL East.

The Dodgers took the first two games, 3–0 and 5–2, behind the strong pitching of Don Sutton and Andy Messersmith, with Mike Marshall in relief. Pittsburgh came roaring back in the third game, as Richie Hebner and Willie Stargell each hit home runs and drove in six runs between them. Those who expected Pittsburgh to continue their comeback in the fourth game were sadly disappointed. Sutton allowed only three hits in seven innings, before deferring to Mike Marshall. Pittsburgh's one run came on another homer by Stargell, but the Dodgers cleaned up on the Pirates' pitchers for 12 runs on 12 hits, including two home runs by Steve Garvey.

Sutton, the star of the playoff, gave up only one earned run over 17 innings and recorded two of the Dodgers' wins. L.A.'s pitching staff had a collective 2.00 ERA in the four-game series and held Pittsburgh to a .194 batting average. The big question now was whether they could shut down the power of the Oakland A's with the same effectiveness.

1974 WORLD SERIES

	W	L
Oakland (AL)	4	1
Los Angeles (NL)	1	4

The 1974 World Series was the first one to pit two West Coast teams against each other. Writers and fans alike watched in anticipation for the clash between California's two cultures and, on a less cerebral level, between the two best teams in baseball.

The confrontation was between two clubs that seemed to be evenly matched in all departments. The powerful bats of Steve Garvey, Jim Wynn, and Bill Buckner were matched by those of their neighbors to the north: Reggie Jackson, Joe Rudi, and Sal Bando. Both pitching staffs were excellent, and both teams had speed: Davey Lopes had stolen 59 bases for L.A., and Bill North had stolen 53 for Oakland.

The matter to be resolved was how the youth of the Dodgers would fare against the experience of the A's, appearing in their third World Series in a row. The Dodger infield, Steve Garvey, Davey Lopes, Bill Russell, and Ron Cey, averaged 26 years of age with less than five years of major-league experience, and none had ever appeared in the October classic. Lopes and Steve Yeager, the man behind the plate, were finishing only their third year in the major leagues.

The first game saw Andy Messersmith, a 20-game winner, go to the mound against Oakland's Ken Holtzman, winner of 59 games over the three previous seasons. Ken Holtzman is a pitcher who seldom hit his weight, and he is a slim man at that. Because of the DH rule in the American League, Holtzman had not come to bat all season, but he still managed to repeat what he had done twice in the 1973 World Series, namely hit a double, as he helped win the opener with his bat. Holtzman went to third on a wild pitch and scored on a suicide bunt laid down by Bert Campaneris. Why Dark made the decision to bunt on a two-and-two count and why Walt Alston did not call for a pitchout still have the second-guessers arguing this game.

Vida Blue and Blue Moon Odom matched the six-hitter thrown by Don Sutton, but Joe Ferguson's home run was the margin of difference as L.A. evened up the Series at one game apiece.

Two Dodger home runs were wasted in the third game, as L.A. gave up two unearned runs, giving Oakland its second win and Catfish Hunter his third World Series win in as many years.

The fourth game saw the bat of Ken Holtzman again emerge as a factor. He hit a home run, and he and Rollie Fingers allowed only two runs on seven hits.

But the game was won by a pinch hitter who had joined Oakland in midseason after languishing for six and a half years with the Minnesota Twins. Jim Holt had hit .143 for Oakland in 1974, but in the sixth inning of the fourth game, he was about to take his place in history as he came to bat for Ray Fosse, with the bases loaded. He stroked a single to right off Andy Messersmith, and two runs scored. As Wells Twombly of *The San Francisco Examiner* wrote at the time, Jim Holt had never done anything as important before, and he never would again. He shuttled back and forth between Oakland and the Pacific Coast League for the next two years. Twombly wrote, "His round, agreeable face will never be cast in bronze and bolted to the wall at Cooperstown, where baseball stores its holy icons." But, for less than a minute, as Sal Bando scored and as Reggie Jackson slid home, James William Holt was the most important man in baseball.

Joe Rudi's home run off the masterful Mike Marshall in relief broke up a tie in the fifth game to give Oakland its fourth win and its third World Championship in a row. Not since the New York Yankees reigned from 1948 through 1953 had any team managed to win three World Series in a row. Ironically, three of those Yankee wins came at the expense of the Dodgers, the team from Brooklyn made immortal by Roger Kahn as the boys of summer.

For the third year in a row, no pitcher was able to throw a complete game. Four of the five games were settled by 3–2 scores, and Rollie Fingers appeared in four games in relief. With each passing year, the bullpen was becoming an increasingly important part of baseball.

The question of whether experience would prevail over youth was settled in the affirmative. It was not overwhelming hitting or dominating pitching that won the Series as much as total team play; the combination of what fans call proper execution as well as the ability to capitalize on the other team's errors. For the young Los Angeles club, this would be only the first of three appearances in the World Series in the 1970s. A healthy Tommy John might have made the difference for the Dodgers, but he of the bionic arm, after an outstanding 13–3 beginning, sat out the last half of the 1974 season. His comeback, and that of the Dodgers, was a few years away.

1974 QUIZ

1. Who became the seventh player to steal two bases in one inning in World Series play?
2. Who was the Oakland player who became the fourteenth pitcher to hit a home run in a World Series game?
3. Who was the Dodger infielder who tied the World Series record by hitting eight singles in a five-game Series?
4. Who became the seventh player to be hit by a pitch three times in total World Series play?
5. Who was the pitcher who set a new record of appearing in the most games in relief in total World Series play, by pitching in four games in this Series?
6. Who was the Oakland outfielder who became the eighth man to play three different positions in one Series?
7. Who tied Bucky Harris's 50-year-old record for second basemen by making eight putouts in a nine-inning game?
8. Who set a new record for relief pitchers by appearing in all five games of a 5-game Series?
9. Who was the Oakland second baseman who set a new record for most double plays in a 5-game Series and most double plays started in a game?

1975 CHAMPIONSHIP SERIES

American League

	W	L
Boston (East)	3	0
Oakland (West)	0	3

National League

	W	L
Cincinnati (West)	3	0
Pittsburgh (East)	0	3

When the A's finished easily ahead of Kansas City, winning their fifth consecutive Western Division championship, it looked like still another trip to the World Series for an Oakland club that was beginning to seem invincible. Boston won its division, thanks largely to the herculean effort of Fred Lynn, Rookie of the Year as well as MVP. Experts did not feel that, all things considered, New England's Red Sox were a solid enough club to wrest the AL pennant away from the West Coast show now known as Finley's Follies.

The experts were wrong, and Boston captured its first pennant in 18 years. Solid hitting at the right time and a superior pitching performance by the Red Sox staff gave them a surprising three-game sweep of the World Champions. Oakland could manage only one home run and a measly seven runs in the three-game series. Luis Tiant, finishing another good season, went all the way in the first game, hurling a three-hitter. Lynn was joined by Carl Yastrzemski and Carlton Fisk in providing all the offensive firepower that was needed. Ken Holtzman and Rollie Fingers, the heroes of so many big games to date, took the three losses.

A resurgent Cincinnati club had gotten its Big Red Machine back in gear, swamping Los Angeles in the NL Western Division. Joe Morgan, Johnny Bench, Pete Rose, and Tony Perez had great seasons in 1975. The speedy little Joe Morgan hit .327, with 94 RBIs; Pete Rose hit .317, with 210 hits and a league-leading 47 doubles; Johnny Bench hit 28 home runs and had 110 RBIs; Tony Perez hit 20 home runs and had 109 RBIs. There were also Ken Griffey's .305 batting average and George Foster's 23 home runs to contend with. As a team, they had produced 840 runs, over 100 more than the winners of the Eastern Division, the Pittsburgh Pirates.

Pittsburgh, however, was not a team to be taken lightly. They had a slugging average even higher than Cincinnati's, and they had five men in the lineup who had hit over 15 home runs in 1975, namely Richie Hebner, Al Oliver, Richie Zisk, Willie Stargell, and Dave Parker.

In the midst of all this power, the only home run hit in the first game came from an unlikely source: Don Gullett. Gullett had never hit one before in six regular seasons of play. He also had a single and three RBIs in all to go with a complete game as the Reds won the opener 8–3. Perez, Rose, Concepcion, and Oliver hit homers in the last two games, as the Cincinnati pitchers held Pittsburgh to a total of five hits. The last game saw a 14-strikeout performance by John Candelaria, the big Pirate rookie, go for nought. Cincinnati had swept Pittsburgh in three games.

The encounter between the Boston Red Sox and the Cincinnati Reds was anticipated with less than glee by American League fans. In addition to their awesome offensive power, the Reds had led the National League in fielding and, heaven help Carlton Fisk, they had also led the National League in stolen bases, copping over 100 more than Boston.

The most optimistic thing that one could say was that the pitching staffs seemed evenly matched. Neither team had a 20-game winner, but both teams had great depth in their rosters. When the Big Red Machine saw the Green Monster at Fenway Park, technicolor fireworks would surely be the result.

1975 WORLD SERIES

	W	L
Cincinnati (NL)	4	3
Boston (AL)	3	4

In spite of what appeared to many as a mismatch, the 1975 World Series turned out to be one of the most evenly played, one of the most exciting, action-packed classics in many years. To describe a Series that went seven games with the winners scoring 29 runs on 59 hits to the losers' 30 runs on 60 hits as evenly played may be an understatement. To call a series that was still not decided with two outs in the top of the ninth inning of the last game exciting is hardly an exaggeration. To label a series that saw a record 6 home runs in one game and 13 in all as action-packed is beating the obvious.

This Series featured, at one time or another, everything that baseball has to offer: great individual efforts, spectacular fielding, daring base running, and one of the great controversies for which the World Series is known.

In the opening game, Cincinnati sent young Don Gullett to the mound to oppose one of Cuba's gifts to baseball, the ageless Luis Tiant. El Tiante stroked a single and scored, while pitching a complete game, a shutout on five hits.

The cold rain of the second game at Fenway did not dampen the hustle of Dave Concepcion. With two outs and behind by a run, Concepcion rejected the ugly thought of making the last out in two games in a row. Instead he hit a single to score Bench from second. He then stole second and scored on Ken Griffey's double. The Reds pulled out a win at the last moment and evened up the Series.

The third game saw a total of ten pitchers give up a record-setting number of six home runs in a seesaw battle that was won in the tenth inning on a bunt. That bunt, and what happened after it, will make this game best remembered as featuring one of the most controversial decisions in World Series history. Some say that it was also one of the biggest mistakes an umpire ever made, one that may very well have cost Boston the World Championship.

The controversy took place in the bottom of the tenth inning with the score tied and Cincinnati at bat. Cesar Geronimo led off with a single, and Ed Armbrister was sent up to pinch-hit for Rawly Eastwick. Armbrister was an outfielder who had come from the Astros as an afterthought in the big trade of 1971 that brought Jack Billingham, Cesar Geronimo, Denis Menke, and Joe Morgan to the Reds. He had labored long and hard in the minor leagues since 1967, but he still had only 65 at-bats in the 1975 season.

The fame that had eluded Ed Armbrister for so long was suddenly his as he laid down a bunt that bounced high in front of the plate. The photos clearly show that Armbrister did not move and Fisk collided with him as he leaped to make what would have been a double play. Instead, Fisk threw wildly into center field after he was forced to push the batter out of his way.

Fisk and Red Sox manager Darrell Johnson claimed interference, but plate umpire Larry Barnett refused to make the call, and first-base umpire Stello sustained him. After the game, the umpires talked about the fact that the batter did not *intentionally* get in the way of the catcher. But Allen Lewis of *The Philadelphia Inquirer* and chairman of the Scoring Rules Committee for a decade said in *Baseball Digest* that they were citing the wrong part of rule 7.09. The debate over this play and the meaning of the rule itself still goes on, but no matter how many words are spent on this play, Ed Armbrister will always be safe and sitting on second. Geronimo went to third on the play and went on to score the winning run when Joe Morgan singled him home.

Anyone who thought that this unfortunate ruling and Boston's consequent loss would take the heart out of the Red Sox club was not familiar with the courage of Señor Tiant. Luis pitched another complete game in the fourth outing and evened the series at two apiece.

In the fifth game, another gift from Cuba, Tony Perez, came out of his 0-for-15 slump with two home runs and four RBIs to get the win for Don Gullett and bring the Reds within one game of winning the Series.

One day of travel and the intervention of Mother Nature in the form of three days of rain allowed Darrell Johnson to call on his blue-chip pitcher one more time. Luis Tiant gave it his best shot, but he was taken out after pitching to one batter in the eighth inning. In the bottom of the eighth, with two out, Bernie Carbo hit a pinch-hit home run with two men on, to tie the score at 6-all. The Sox loaded the bases in the tenth but came up empty. Cincinnati's Joe Morgan was robbed of a home run by Dwight Evans in the eleventh. Finally, in the bottom of the twelfth inning, Carlton Fisk ended the game more than four hours after it began. He hit a shot off the left-field foul pole for a home run. It was one of the most thrilling games in World Series history, and, when it was over, the teams stood at three wins apiece.

The fans at Fenway smelled a win when Don Gullett walked home two runs in the third inning as Boston jumped to a 3–0 lead. Hard base running by Pete Rose and another Perez home run brought the Reds to within one run. A Griffey single and a stolen base and Rose's single brought them all even. Morgan singled home Griffey in the ninth, and the Red Sox went down in order. The Cincinnati Reds had won their second World Series since 1919 and their first in 35 years.

Boston had lost in spite of the great fielding and hitting efforts of Fred Lynn and Dwight Evans, in spite of Carlton Fisk's getting on base 13 times, in spite of Yaz and Rico Petrocelli hitting over .300, and in spite of the magnificent pitching effort by one of baseball's most indomitable characters, Luis Tiant.

The MVP of one of the greatest Series of all time went to one of baseball's greatest players. Pete Rose hit .370, with ten hits, including a double and a triple. He also walked five times. He knocked in two runs and scored three more while playing errorless ball.

The Reds stole six bases while Boston stole none, but speed did not decide this World Series. Neither did the Green Monster. The narrowest of margins decided this World Series—a bunt by Ed Armbrister and a call that will give us all fuel for the fire of the Hot Stove League.

1975 QUIZ

1. Who had the highest batting average of all Red Sox players and became only the second man in history to hit two pinch-hit home runs in one World Series?

2. Who was the Cincinnati first baseman who came out of his hitting slump to become only the thirteenth player in World Series history to hit back-to-back home runs in the same game?
3. Who were the two Boston outfielders who set a new record for a seven-game Series by accepting 24 chances without making an error?
4. Who was the Boston player who made three errors, tying the record for second basemen in a seven-game Series?
5. Who was the Cincinnati player who made an unassisted double play, only the ninth such play by a first baseman in World Series history?
6. Who would rather forget that he tied the record for catchers by making two errors?
7. When Cincinnati hit back-to-back home runs in the fifth inning of game three, they became only the seventh team in World Series history to have consecutive home runs in one inning. Who were the two home-run hitters?
8. Who was the relief pitcher who became the fifth player in World Series history to win two games while losing none?
9. Pitchers have started three games in a seven-game Series 37 times, the last time being in this Series. Who were the two pitchers—one with Boston and one with Cincinnati—who started three games each in this Series?
10. Who had the highest batting average of any Red Sox player who had at least twenty at-bats?

1976 CHAMPIONSHIP SERIES

American League	W	L	*National League*	W	L
New York (East)	3	2	Cincinnati (West)	3	0
Kansas City (West)	2	3	Philadelphia (East)	0	3

In Billy Martin's first year as manager of the New York Yankees, he took his club to first place in the Eastern Division, 10½ games ahead of the Baltimore Orioles. In the West, Whitey Herzog, also in his first full year as manager of the Kansas City Royals, led his club to first place, edging out the Oakland A's by 2½ games. Oakland had had their days in the sun and, for them, the rest of the 1970s was to be an abysmal failure. Charlie Finley traded away or sold one player after another, and for the rest of the decade, they would never again finish better than 23 games out of first place.

The Yankees were led by their captain, Thurman Munson, who was the AL MVP of the year, and Graig Nettles, the AL home-run champ. Between them, they had 49 home runs and 198 RBIs. They were favored over a Kansas City club that boasted the leading hitter in baseball, George Brett.

Catfish Hunter, one of the many refugees from Oakland, won the opening game on a brilliant five-hitter. The Royals and the Yankees took turns winning the next three games, and the playoff went down to the wire. With the game tied at six apiece in the bottom of the ninth inning of game five, Chris Chambliss hit Mark Littell's first pitch over the right-field fence. It was the most dramatic ending yet to a playoff.

It was the first pennant for the Yankees in 12 years, and the fans went wild. By the time Chambliss got to second base, it had been ripped up, and he never actually got to home plate. Once again, the fans had let their enthusiasm get the best of them. When the celebration/riot was over, the house that Ruth built was damaged to the tune of $100,000.

Danny Ozark's Philadelphia Phillies ran away with the Eastern Division of the NL, giving them the honor of facing the Cincinnati Reds, again the victors of the NL West. In what sounded like a tennis score, the Reds won handily in three games: 6–3, 6–2, 7–6. The Phillies were on top 6–4 as they went into the bottom of the ninth of the third game, but their hopes were quickly crushed as the first two batters, George Foster and Johnny Bench, hit back-to-back home runs.

After a 15-year hiatus, the Cincinnati Reds were again going to meet the New York Yankees in the World Series.

1976 WORLD SERIES

	W	L
Cincinnati (NL)	4	0
New York (AL)	0	4

When New York and Cincinnati had last met in the World Series in 1961, the Yankees won it 4–1. In that Series, Whitey Ford, coming off one of the best seasons in his great career, pitched 14 innings of shutout ball while walking only one man. The Chairman of the Board ran his record of scoreless innings in World Series play to 32, surpassing Babe Ruth's old record. In that series, the Yankees had a pretty fair one-two punch in Roger Maris and Mickey Mantle, while the Reds had two outfielders—Frank Robinson and Vada Pinson—who had hit .323 and .343, respectively.

But that was then. In this Series, Cincinnati was to get their long-awaited revenge. The defending champions were loaded with power, and they used it as they swept the Yankees in four straight. They pounded Yankee pitching for 22 runs, while allowing only 8.

This was the first World Series to use the designated hitter, presumably as a concession to the American League. It didn't help the Yankees very much, as their various DHs—Carlos May, Elliot Maddox, and Lou Piniella—managed only one hit in the four games. On the other hand, the young Dan Driessen hit .357 as the Reds' lone DH.

Catfish Hunter had pitched 12 innings in the playoffs, and he was too tired to open the World Series. Billy Martin reached into his less than outstanding staff and chose Doyle Alexander to pitch the opening game. Alexander had come from Baltimore as part of the big trade that had also brought Ken Holtzman, Grant Jackson, and Elrod Hendricks to the Yankees. He had just finished the best season of his life, winning 13 and losing 9. Alexander allowed five runs before leaving in the seventh inning, and the Yankees could manage only one run.

Hunter pitched a strong game in the second outing, but the game was lost in the bottom of the ninth. Dan Driessen, the Reds' DH, put on a one-man show in the third game, as he walked, singled, doubled, and homered, scoring two runs as the Reds won 6–2.

Johnny Bench put the icing on the cake in the fourth and final game with a three-run home run as the Yankees were disposed of, 5–1. Bench was named MVP, knocking in 6 of his team's 21 runs. He went 8 for 14, batting .533, with a double, a triple, and two home runs. Bench's rival and Yankee counterpart, Thurman Munson, put on a brave show himself, getting nine singles in 17 at-bats for a .529 batting average.

The 1976 World Series was as dull as the one before it was exciting. Before the Yankees got into it, they were out of it. As examples of the kinds of stories that the sportswriters jumped on in the midst of their boredom, consider these two items. The Yankees had been using walkie-talkies in the stands throughout the season to assist them in their positioning of the outfielders, and Bowie Kuhn allowed them to continue the practice in the World Series. The commissioner reversed his decision when it was brought to his attention that the Yankees were using more than one man to do this. He went back to allowing it when the Yankees agreed to revert to the original agreement. Whatever the value of this system during the season, it did not help the New York outfielders much this October.

Billy Martin, perhaps in an effort to wake up his club, was thrown out of the last game for tossing a baseball on the field. When Martin can't think of anything more exciting to do than that, you know that things must really be dull.

Not since John McGraw's Giants had beaten Miller Huggins's Yankees in the 1921 and 1922 World Series had a National League team won two straight world titles.

1976 QUIZ

1. Who struck out three times as a pinch-hitter, tying the record held by Gabby Hartnett (1929) and Rollie Helmsley (1932)?
2. Who was the Cincinnati outfielder who tied Luis Aparicio's 1966 record of getting caught stealing the most times in a four-game Series?
3. Who tied a World Series record held by only three other players by getting seven hits in a row in two consecutive games? He went on to hit .529 in the Series.
4. Who was the Dodgers third baseman who became only the thirteenth player to lead off a World Series game with a home run?

5. Who was the Yankee shortstop who became only the fourteenth player in history to hit a home run in his first World Series at-bat?
6. Who was the Yankee—a former Rookie of the Year—who became the thirty-sixth player in World Series history to get four hits in one game?
7. Who were the two Cincinnati players who each tied the record of stealing the most bases (two) in a four-game Series, a record set by Charlie Deal and Rabbit Maranville in 1914?
8. Who was the Cincinnati catcher who became only the twenty-fourth player in World Series history to hit two consecutive home runs in the same game?
9. Who was the Cincinnati player who tied the record for outfielders by making eight putouts in a nine-inning game?
10. Who set a new record for a four-game Series by throwing out five runners attempting to steal?

1977 CHAMPIONSHIP SERIES

American League

	W	L
New York (East)	3	2
Kansas City (West)	2	3

National League

	W	L
Los Angeles (West)	3	1
Philadelphia (East)	1	3

The Yankees came from behind late in the season to pass the Red Sox, and they held on through September for their second straight win in the Eastern Division of the AL. In the West, the Kansas City Royals again breezed to first place, eight games ahead of the Texas Rangers. The Rangers managed second place in spite of having four different managers during the year.

The Yankee team that met the Royals was not the same one that had gotten blown out in the last World Series. Reggie Jackson had joined them as a free agent after Finley traded him to Baltimore; a rejuvenated Sparky Lyle had won the Cy Young Award; a young Ron Guidry had just finished a great season, his first in the major leagues; Mike Torrez had been traded from Oakland and won 17 games; Mickey Rivers had just put together the best season of his career, hitting .326.

Surprisingly, the Royals proved to be much harder competitors this year. They played aggressively and hard, and Paul Splittorff won the first game 7–2. The Yankees, angered by a block put on Willie Randolph by Hal McRae during a routine force play, won the second game 6–2, as rookie Ron Guidry pitched a complete game, a strong three-hitter. The Royals won the third with a four-hitter by their 20-game winner, Dennis Leonard. The Yankees came back in the fourth, setting up the deciding game to be played at Royals Stadium in Kansas City.

In the first inning of the last game, George Brett slid hard into Graig Nettles and came up swinging, emptying both dugouts. Order was soon restored, and the game went on. In the top of the ninth, the Yankees were behind by two runs, but they scored twice, winning their second straight pennant. In the midst of their victory, however, New York was worried about Reggie Jackson, who was in a terrible slump. He could manage only two singles in 16 at-bats and had been benched for Paul Blair. The Yankees would need Reggie's bat in the World Series.

In Tom La Sorda's first season as manager, the Los Angeles Dodgers waltzed to a ten-game lead in the NL west and faced Danny Ozark's Philadelphia Phillies, the leader of the Eastern Division for the second year in a row. Each team had good pitching, and each had a legitimate contender for the Cy Young Award: The Phillies' Steve Carlton had a 23–10 record while the Dodgers' Tommy John was 20–7. The Phillies had Mike Schmidt, who had averaged 38 home runs a season for the last four years, but this year the Dodgers were the first team in history with four players who had 30 or more home runs. Steve Garvey, Reggie Smith, Dusty Baker, and Ron Cey had 125 homers among them.

The two pitching aces, Carlton and John, went head to head in the opening game. John left the game after four unearned runs were scored. Ron Cey brought the Dodgers to within one run with a grand-slam home run, but the Phillies scored two more times and won the first game 7–5.

The Dodgers won the second on a complete game from Don Sutton and another grand-slam home run, this one by Dusty Baker. The third game was settled in the favor of Los Angeles in the top of the ninth inning on a bad call. Photos show that Davey Lopes was out on a play at first base, but umpire Bruce Froemming called him safe. If he had been called out, the game would have been over. Instead, he went on to score the game-winning run.

John went against Carlton again in the fourth game, and Dusty Baker's two-run homer was all John needed as he went all the way, giving up only one run.

For the first time since 1963, the Los Angeles Dodgers would meet the New York Yankees in the World Series, renewing an old and intense rivalry.

1977 WORLD SERIES

	W	L
New York (AL)	4	2
Los Angeles (NL)	2	4

When fighters with similar styles meet each other, the result is usually a boring bout. But when two great baseball teams with the same kinds of strengths meet each other, the result is usually dynamite. The New York Yankees and the Los Angeles Dodgers were both great teams with comparable strengths.

Each team had power. Over the 1977 season, the Yankees had hit 184 home runs, while the Dodgers had 191. Each team had good pitching, with the slight edge going to Los Angeles. Each team had a stopper in the bullpen: Sparky Lyle with 26 saves for the Yankees and Charlie Hough with 22 saves for Los Angeles. Both teams had individual superstars, and both had great depth as well. In a best-of-seven Series, with two teams so evenly matched, the deciding factor could be the man who got the hot hand.

In the first game, Billy Martin surprised everyone by nominating Don Gullett to pitch against Dodger ace Don Sutton. Gullett had been on the disabled list for almost all of August, and he had been hit hard in the two innings he pitched in the playoff. Nevertheless, he pitched a strong game, and he and Sparky Lyle gave up only three runs on six hits over 12 innings. Willie Randolph got the hot hand in this game, blasting a two-run homer and scoring the next two runs as well, after getting a walk and a double.

Martin went to another sore-armed pitcher, Catfish Hunter, in the second game, but this time his strategy backfired. Hunter got tagged for three quick home runs, and the Dodgers drew the Series even behind a complete game by Burt Hooton.

In the third and fourth outings, the Yankees got complete games from two of their pitching stars: Mike Torrez and Ron Guidry. In winning 5–3 and 4–2, they held the Dodgers to a total of 11 hits. The Dodgers roared back in the fifth game, scoring ten runs to support Don Sutton's complete game.

The teams returned to New York for the sixth game at Yankee Stadium. Those who saw the game saw one of the most memorable, most prodigious, most awesome displays of power in World Series history. A lot of players came up with hot hands over the years, but no one, absolutely no one, ever came up with as hot a hand as Reggie Jackson did on Tuesday evening, October 18, 1977.

Burt Hooton walked Reggie Jackson in the second inning, perhaps remembering that he had hit a home run thc last time up, in the fifth game. They should have walked Jackson all night. Chris Chambliss hit a home run, scoring Reggie, and the score was tied at 2-all. In the top of the third, Reggie Smith hit a home run to put the Dodgers ahead again, but at that point, the Series was essentially over for Los Angeles.

In the fourth inning, Reggie came to bat with a man on and hit the first pitch served to him into the seats. In the fifth inning, Reggie came to bat again with a man on, and he again hit the first pitch served to him into the seats.

When Reggie came to bat in the eighth inning, he was greeted by one of the greatest ovations of his career and one of the loudest in Yankee history. Jackson, always one to warm up to a good crowd, responded by hitting the first pitch offered to him into the seats. This time, the ball went into the cheap seats as the blast was estimated at some 450 feet.

In three swings of the bat, Reggie had tied or broken virtually every hitting record in World Series history. His virtuoso performance was so overwhelming that all other performances paled by comparison. Forgotten will be the fact that the Dodgers hit nine home runs to the Yankees eight or the fact that they had two more hits and scored two more runs in the Series; forgotten will be the five RBIs each by Steve Yeager, Dusty Baker, and Reggie Smith and the four RBIs of Chris Chambliss; forgotten will be the nine hits of Steve Garvey.

And for Reggie Jackson, at least for a little while, forgotten would be a year of turmoil and strife in which he was benched in the playoff. It would be hard to forget the humiliating day in Boston when Billy Martin accused him of dogging it in the field and literally dragged him into the dugout before a TV audience of millions. They almost came to blows that day, but a proud and professional Reggie Jackson, reinstalled as a cleanup hitter, went on to carry the Yankees on his back for the rest of the season, all the way to a World Championship.

In 1977, Reggie often doubted his decision to come to New York. But he was certainly right about one thing: They did name a candy bar after him.

1977 QUIZ

1. Who had the highest slugging average in a six-game Series of any player in history?
2. In the sixth game, Reggie Jackson tied a Series record held by only four men: Babe Ruth, Earle Combs, Frank Crosetti, and Enos Slaughter. What was that record?
3. Who set a new record by scoring ten runs in a six-game Series?
4. Who was the Yankee center fielder and lead-off hitter who became the fourth man in World Series history to go 0 for 6 in an extra-inning game?
5. Who set a new record for third basemen by making 20 assists in a six-game Series?
6. Who was the Yankee outfielder who set a new record for a six-game Series by accepting 25 chances without an error?
7. When the Yankees hit back-to-back home runs in the eighth inning of game five, they were only the eighth team in World Series history to have consecutive home runs in one inning. Who were the two home-run hitters?
8. Who tied the record last accomplished in 1959 of winning two games while losing none in a 6-game Series?
9. Who was the catcher who tied the record of one or more hits in each game of a 6-game Series?
10. Who was the Dodger from the 1950s whose record was broken when Reggie Jackson logged sixteen extra bases on long hits?

1978 CHAMPIONSHIP SERIES

American League

	W	L
New York (East)	3	1
Kansas City (West)	1	3

National League

	W	L
Los Angeles (West)	3	1
Philadelphia (East)	1	3

The Boston Red Sox had won first place in the AL East by the end of July, by which time they had buried the Yankees. The only problem was that they'd forgotten to tell the Yankees and their new manager, Bob Lemon.

New York started to come back in August, and in September they passed a slumping Red Sox club. From September 1 until the day they beat Boston in a playoff game, the Yankees posted a 22–9 record, while Boston went 15–15.

On October 2, at Fenway Park, Bucky Dent faced his former teammate, Mike Torrez, with two men on base and behind by two runs. After fouling off the first pitch, Mickey Rivers sent out a new bat because the one Dent was using had cracked.

Dent was hardly a home-run threat, having hit fewer than two dozen homers in his major-league career. He hit the next pitch over the left-field wall. The Sox came back but a Jackson home run shut the door and gave the Yankees their third win in a row in the Eastern Division.

They met Kansas City, winner by five games in the West, for the third time in a row to battle for the AL pennant.

Reggie Jackson walked twice, singled, doubled, and homered in the opening game. He knocked in three and scored two as the Yankees won 7–1.

Kansas City raked Ed Figueroa, Dick Tidrow, and Sparky Lyle for 16 hits in the second game, to win 10–4 and to even up the Series at one apiece.

George Brett hit three home runs off Catfish Hunter in the third game, but the Yankees still won 6–5, thanks to homers by Munson and Jackson.

Dennis Leonard and Ron Guidry dueled for eight innings in game four. Two of the four hits given up by Leonard were home runs to Graig Nettles and Roy White, and that was enough. Goose Gossage came in to retire the side in the bottom of the ninth, and the Yankees won 2–1, game and pennant.

In the National League it was almost a replay of 1977, as Los Angeles, best of the West, beat the Philadelphia Phillies, three games to one. Steve Garvey hit a triple and two homers to help win the first game 9–5. Lopes hit a triple and a homer in the second game behind Tommy John's four-hitter.

Steve Carlton stymied a Dodger sweep by pitching a complete game and knocking in four runs as well.

The Dodgers won the final game in the tenth inning. The Phillies had blown one big chance in the first inning, when they loaded up the bases with no outs but couldn't score a run. They blew their last chance in the tenth inning, when Garry Maddox misplayed a Dusty Baker line drive. Bill Russell took the moment and singled home the winning run.

The Dodgers had earned the right to face the Yankees in the World Series again, and to make up for their loss in 1977.

1978 WORLD SERIES

	W	L
New York (AL)	4	2
Los Angeles (NL)	2	4

In the 1978 World Series, the names were the same but the casts were slightly different. The Yankees had been hard hit by injuries and consequently did not appear as strong as they were when they last faced the Dodgers in 1977. Willie Randolph, the solid second baseman, had been playing hurt for months, but he was out for good by the time the Series started. Don Gullett, a 14-game winner in 1977, had spent most of the season on the disabled list, pitching only 45 innings. Mickey Rivers, the speed demon, couldn't run, and Thurman Munson, the catcher, couldn't throw. Chris Chambliss, the powerful first baseman, appeared in only half the games and went a sickly 2 for 11.

On the other hand, both clubs were stronger in the bullpen thanks to the free-agency draft. Each team had picked up an excellent reliever who had spent the previous year with Pittsburgh. L.A. got Terry Forster, their club leader with five wins and 22 saves; New York got Goose Gossage, their club leader with ten wins and 27 saves.

In the opening game, four Yankee pitchers gave up 11 runs on 15 hits, including two home runs by Davey Lopes. Los Angeles also won the second game, which will be remembered for the dramatic duel that ended the ninth inning. With two men on and two outs, down by one run, Reggie Jackson worked young Bob Welch to a full count. One swing of Jackson's bat could put the Yankees ahead by two runs. Welch delivered and the runners took off, but there was no joy in New York. Mighty Reggie had struck out.

An unusually shaky Ron Guidry went all the way to win game three in spite of giving up eight hits and seven bases on balls. Guidry owed his win to Graig Nettles, who put on one of the all-time greatest fielding performances in history. Nettles flung his body to the left and to the right, making one play after another, each seeming to be even more impossible than the one before. Two of his great plays came with the bases loaded, and he robbed the Dodgers of at least five runs. Reggie Smith summed it up when he said, "It's Dodgers two, Nettles one."

Some say that the third game was the turning point of the Series, while many others say that it was the fourth. It would probably be most accurate to say that those two games coming back to back, beating L.A. aces Don Sutton and Tommy John, broke the hearts of the Dodgers.

Some players just seem to attract action, or perhaps it is that wherever they are, so is the action. Reggie Jackson is certainly one of these players, maybe even the outstanding example. The sixth inning of the fourth game saw Reggie at center stage again. With one out, he had just knocked in a run; Munson was on second; Reggie was on first. Lou Piniella hit a liner to Bill Russell at shortstop, and Russell caught the ball and then dropped it. Russell says that he did not drop the ball on purpose but, by doing so, he greatly increased his chance to get a double play to end the inning. He picked up the ball and touched second, forcing Jackson. Russell then threw to first to double up Piniella. Reggie threw out a hip as though he was practicing for the world's hula-hoop championship. The ball bounced off Reggie into fair territory and, while Steve Garvey was arguing about it, Thurman Munson raced home. Give Reggie's hip one RBI.

The first-base umpire ruled no interference, and the second-base umpire said that he didn't see the play. For the second time in four years, a key play in a key game hinged on a judgment call as to whether there was intentional interference. They ought either to change the wording of that rule or teach umpires how to read minds.

In the fifth game, Jim Beattie, a youngster from Dartmouth, pitched his first complete major-league game to bring the Yankees ahead in the Series three games to two. The Yankees scored 12 runs on 18 hits, 16 of them singles. The Dodgers committed three errors and looked sloppy in the field.

Hunter and Gossage held the Dodgers to two runs in the sixth game. Bucky Dent and Brian Doyle had five of New York's RBIs, and the Yankees had won their second straight World Championship.

When posterity examines the box scores for this World Series, it will note a .438 batting average for Brian Doyle and wonder who he was. For the sake of posterity and those with short memories, Doyle was a short, skinny 24-year-old who had spent the last six years in Geneva, Gastonia, Pittsfield, Lynchburg, San Antonio, Sacramento, Tacoma, and Columbus. It would be fair to say that he paid his dues before achieving his moment of glory in 1978.

The Series MVP was Bucky Dent, the surehanded little shortstop who plays baseball the way most big men wish they could play it. He hit .417, with ten hits, more than any other Yankee, and he had seven RBIs. Dent and Doyle held down the middle of the Yankee infield, playing brilliant defense.

The two teams set a new record for the most hits (120) in a six-game series. Don Sutton broke one record by allowing ten runs in a six-game series and tied another one by losing two games. Graig Nettles's sparkling performance at third earned him the records of the highest fielding average (1,000), with 26 chances in six games, also the highest ever. He started three double plays, bringing his career total to six, both new records.

Reggie Jackson was hit by the ball three times, once by pitcher Bert Hooton and once by Terry Forster. The third time was by shortstop Bill Russell, and that helped win a game and maybe a World Series.

1978 QUIZ

1. His performance in this Series gave him the highest slugging percentage of all players who appeared in 20 or more games. Who was he?

2. Who was the Dodger infielder who, in game two, became only the third man in World Series history to bat in all four of his club's runs?
3. Who was the Dodgers' lead-off hitter who became only the fourteenth player in World Series history to hit back-to-back home runs in the same game?
4. Who tied Lou Gehrig's record of at least one RBI in eight World Series games in a row?
5. Who was the Dodger pitcher who set a new record by giving up ten runs in a 6-game Series?
6. Who set a new lifetime record for double plays by a third baseman in this Series?
7. Who set a new lifetime record for giving up the most World Series home runs?
8. Who was the Dodger catcher who tied the record by making three putouts in one inning?
9. The Dodgers tied the 6-game record by having three wild pitches. Who threw them?
10. Who was the Yankee DH who was twice hit by a pitch?

1979 CHAMPIONSHIP SERIES

American League	W	L	*National League*	W	L
Baltimore (East)	3	1	Pittsburgh (East)	3	0
California (West)	1	3	Cincinnati (West)	0	3

Baltimore clinched the AL Eastern Division championship on September 22, and coasted to first place, eight games ahead of Milwaukee. The Orioles had been in first place since May.

The California Angels were also in first place for most of the season, and they finished three games ahead of Kansas City. The Angels won 88 games under Jim Fregosi; this was their best record in 19 years, and it was the first time they had finished in first place.

The heart of the club—Don Baylor, Bobby Grich, Rick Miller, and Fred Patek—were all free agents signed by their colorful owner, Gene Autry. The premier hitter of the American League, Rod Carew, was acquired through a trade in 1979, as were Al Cowens and Bert Campaneris. Baylor was the AL MVP, and he led both leagues with 120 runs and 139 RBIs.

Autry and Fregosi had put together quite a team, but they were going up against a Baltimore club that had won 102 games and had a better pitching staff.

In the first game, Jim Palmer lasted nine innings, and John Lowenstein hit a three-run homer in the tenth to give Baltimore the win.

Cy Young Award winner Mike Flanagan won the second game as the Orioles stroked 11 hits and got ten runs to California's eight.

Frank Tanana and Don Aase combined for a 4–3 win in the third game, but the Orioles wrapped it up in the fourth game. Scott McGregor pitched a shutout, while Baltimore amassed eight runs.

Pittsburgh and Cincinnati were both in second place at the end of July, but they were in first when it counted, at the end of the season.

The Pirates swept the series in three games: 5–2, 3–2, and 7–1. The Pittsburgh pitchers held the mighty Cincinnati bats to 23 hits in 107 at-bats, a .215 batting average.

Pops Stargell hit .455, with six RBIs. He hit a three-run homer in the eleventh inning of the first game; he hit a single and a double in the second, and a homer and a double in the finale.

He was named MVP of the playoff, and he avenged, in the best way he knew how, the three encounters with Cincinnati in 1970, 1972, and 1975. The Reds had the edge in those playoffs nine games to two and kept Pittsburgh out of three World Series.

The final World Series of the decade would match the Baltimore Orioles against the Pittsburgh Pirates. It was Baltimore's third appearance in the 1970s and Pittsburgh's second.

1979 WORLD SERIES

	W	L
Pittsburgh (NL)	4	3
Baltimore (AL)	3	4

The first game of the 76th World Series did not start until a day after it was supposed to, and that set the tone for this meeting between Baltimore and Pittsburgh. The first game set a new record as the longest nine-inning night game, and the fourth game set a new record as the longest nine-inning day game. The Series lasted seven games, from October 9, when the first game was to be played, until October 17, but with the cold wet weather helping to set the mood, it somehow seemed longer.

Neither team looked sharp, as 18 errors were committed, 10 by Pittsburgh and 8 by Baltimore. The winner turned out to be the club that did a few more things correctly and fewer things wrong.

After falling behind three games to one, Pittsburgh became only the fourth team to come back and win the last three. Oriole manager Earl Weaver, generally regarded as having one of the best baseball minds around, has been accused by some of misusing his pitching staff.

An examination of the box scores does give the impression that the fact that a DH was not used in this series caused him some problems. Pinch hitters seemed to have been used prematurely, and pitchers who were still doing the job were yanked.

After all, Baltimore did have the best pitching staff in baseball in 1979. They had the lowest ERA; Dennis Martinez was the most durable pitcher; Mike Flanagan and Scott McGregor were surely among the top ten pitchers in the league. Jim Palmer, on the disabled list for a month, had his worst year in a long time, but Don Stanhouse had seven wins and over 20 saves. This staff, with Steve Stone and Tim Stoddard as well, should have been able to hold the Pittsburgh Pirates to something less than the highest batting and slugging averages for a winning team in World Series history.

Palmer was still pitching well in the seventh inning of game two when he left the game for a pinch hitter, Pat Kelly. Stanhouse lost the game in relief. In the fifth game, Flanagan was also lifted for pinch-hitter Kelly in spite of the fact that he had a 2–1 lead at the time. Pittsburgh unloaded on Baltimore relievers Stoddard, Martinez, and Stanhouse, to win 7–1. In the seventh and final game, McGregor was losing 2–0 when he was yanked for a pinch hitter and the ninth inning was pathetically pitched by 5 Orioles in relief.

Lee May, who had 68 RBIs in 117 games with Baltimore as a DH, had only one official at-bat in this Series. Weaver used 9 pinch hitters in all and 9 pitchers as well, in spite of the fact that he got complete games out of Flanagan in the opener and McGregor in the third game. Desperately in need of hitting, Weaver played Kiko Garcia instead of Mark Belanger, who was a better fielder. Garcia responded by hitting .400 but he let a ground ball past him in the last game which may have cost Baltimore the Series.

But it would be unfair to lay the entire blame for the World Series loss at the feet of Earl Weaver. Doug DeCinces hit only .200; Eddie Murray hit .154; Al Bumbry hit .143; Gary Roenicke hit .125. The team batting average was .212 and that tells the tale as well as anything else.

Pops Stargell, with a .400 batting average and seven RBIs, snatched the Series MVP away from Kent Tekulve, who set a new record with his three saves. Pittsburgh's bats hammered out a new record as 5 different players got 10 or more hits.

Earl Weaver's Orioles opened the decade by beating Cincinnati in the World Series 4 games to 1. Say what you will about the managerial miscues of this Series, the fact remains that Weaver was the only man in the major leagues to end the decade managing the same team with which he started the decade.

1979 QUIZ

1. Who was the Baltimore infielder who became the fifth man in World Series history to reach first base safely five times in a nine-inning game, while batting 1.000?
2. Who were the four players—three from Pittsburgh and one from Baltimore—who became the thirty-seventh, thirty-eighth, thirty-ninth, and fortieth players in history to get four hits in one game?
3. Who tied Reggie Jackson's record of 25 total bases in one Series?
4. Who was the Baltimore third baseman who became only the fifteenth player in history to hit a home run in his first World Series at-bat?
5. Who was the Pittsburgh outfielder who tied the record of the most at-bats (33) of any player in a seven-game Series?
6. Who was the Pittsburgh infielder who tied Pepper Martin (1931) and Johnny Lindell (1947) for the highest batting average in a seven-game Series?
7. By drawing four bases on balls in the fourth game, this Oriole infielder became only the fourth player in World Series history to get four free passes in one nine-inning game. Who was he?

8. Who were the two Orioles who each tied a World Series record by appearing in five games as a pinch hitter?
9. Who set a new record for shortstops by making 32 assists in a seven-game Series?
10. Who was the player who set a new record for second basemen by being in on nine double plays in a seven-game Series?
11. Who was the pitcher credited with three saves in one Series, the most of any pitcher in the 1970s?

1970—Answers

1. The pinch hitter was Ty Cline.
2. Dave McNally hit a blast into the left-field bleachers in the third game. He had also homered in the 1969 Series against the Mets. McNally hit the only World Series grand slam of the 1970s.
3. The winner was Tom Phoebus, who came in for Cuellar in relief in the second inning. He gave up no runs and one hit in one and two-thirds innings, that being his total performance for the Series.
4. Paul Blair. Five players held the record before him, starting with Frank Chance in 1908.
5. Lee May accounted for 8 of Cincinnati's 20 runs and hit .389.
6. Paul Blair and Brooks Robinson tied the record last held by the Yankees' Bobby Richardson in 1961.
7. Lee May started two double plays.
8. Lee May and Boog Powell.
9. Brooks Robinson went 4 for 4, including a home run in the fourth game.
10. Paul Blair went 9 for 19, for a .474 batting average.

1971—Answers

1. Willie Stargell, on a hit-and-run play, put on the running exhibition.
2. Jose Pagan, who was alternating at third with Richie Hebner, hit the game-winner.
3. Tom Shopay, Baltimore, went 0 for 4. Only five players before him had pinch-hit in five games.
4. Merv Rettenmund played all three outfield positions. The last player to have held that record was Willie McCovey, who played left field, right field, and first base in 1962.

5. Baltimore had a 2.66 ERA to Pittsburgh's 3.50 ERA.
6. Dobson finished the 1971 season with a 20–8 record and 2.90 ERA. He was not used at all in the playoffs, and Murtaugh did not call on him to pitch until the fourth game of the Series, by which time he had not pitched in two weeks. He struck out three, but walked four and was tagged for ten hits over five and a third innings. He could have started again, but instead he was used for very short relief twice.
7. Brooks Robinson got three singles and two bases on balls in the second game to help lead Baltimore to an 11–3 romp.
8. Frank Robinson was hit twice when he played with Cincinnati. Only six players before him had been hit by a pitch as many times.
9. Merv Rettenmund got two hits in the fifth inning of the second game, contributing to an 11–3 rout of Pittsburgh He was the only player in the 1970s to get two hits in one inning.
10. Powell had fractured his right wrist in August, and he was in great pain during the Series, hitting .111 and getting just one RBI. Many feel that Weaver should have substituted Paul Blair for him in the last five games. As Dave Nightingale of *The Chicago Daily News* summarized it, Buford could have played left, with Blair in center, and Rettenmund moved to right. Frank Robinson could have been moved from right to first. The improvement would have given Baltimore a better glove and arm in center, and a healthier bat in the lineup.

1972—Answers

1. The speedy Allan Lewis had only ten at-bats during the regular season, but he stole eight bases. In 1973, he stole seven bases and scored 16 runs while registering no official at-bats during the regular season, and he was used as a pinch runner three more times in the World Series.
2. Gene Tenace had two home runs to lead Oakland to a 3–2 win in the opening game. He was the only player ever to hit two homers in his first two World Series at-bats.
3. Jack Billingham. Lee May, Tommy Helms, and Jim Stewart went to Houston with him.
4. Tony Perez, who went 0 for 16 in the 1970 Series, hit .435 in this Series. He had eight singles and two doubles in 23 at-bats.

Hal McRae had slightly higher batting average, but he had only nine at-bats.

5. Gonzalo Marquez also tied a World Series record by pinch-hitting in five games. Interestingly, Marquez had played in only 23 games during the regular season, and he was traded to the Cubs the next year.
6. Pete Rose, playing in left field, led off the fifth game by hitting a home run off the first pitch.
7. Cincinnati's Ross Grimsley tied the record last held by the Dodgers' Larry Sherry in 1959. The one game he lost in this Series was as a starter.
8. Jack Billingham for the Reds and Blue Moon Odom for Oakland.
9. Gene Tenace had a slugging average of .913.
10. They were Gonzalo Marquez, Don Mincher, and Angel Mangual.

1973—Answers

1. Willie Mays played in his first World Series as a New York Giant against the Yankees in 1951.
2. Gerry Grote of the Mets joined Heinie (not Honus) Wagner (1912), Johnny Pesky (1946), both with the Red Sox, and Red Schoendienst (1958). However, Grote also set a new record for catchers by accepting 71 chances without making an error.
3. Gene Tenace.
4. Ken Boswell went 3 for 3.
5. Wayne Garrett. Garrett went 5 for 30 in the Series, hitting .167. However, he also became only the twelfth player in World Series history to lead off a game, the third, with a home run.
6. Oakland's Angel Mangual went 0 for 6 in the Series.
7. Reggie Jackson, the Oakland center fielder, went 4 for 6 in the second game, and Rusty Staub, the right fielder for the Mets, went 4 for 4.
8. Felix Millan went hitless in six at-bats in the second game. He went 6 for 32 in the Series, hitting .188. The first two players were Travis Jackson (1924) and Hugh Critz (1933).
9. Rusty Staub led the Mets to a 6–1 win in the fourth game with

three singles, a home run and a base on balls, driving in five runs.

10. Oakland's Darold Knowles pitched six and a third innings in seven games.

1974—Answers

1. Davey Lopes stole two bases in the first inning of the third game, a feat last performed by Lou Brock in 1967 and by no other player in the 1970s.
2. Ken Holtzman hit one over the left-field fence off Andy Messersmith in the fourth game.
3. Steve Garvey.
4. Bert Campaneris was hit twice in the 1973 Series and once in this one.
5. Oakland's Rollie Fingers brought his World Series total to 16 games, breaking his own record.
6. Claudell Washington played all three outfield positions.
7. Davey Lopes made eight putouts in the fourth game, including all three putouts in the sixth inning. Lopes also set the record for most chances accepted by a second baseman, 13, in this game.
8. The Dodgers' Mike Marshall broke Clay Carroll's 1970 record of four games.
9. Dick Green started three double plays in game four and was in on six overall. Joe Gordon was in on five DPs in the 1941 Series and Bill Mazeroski was the last second baseman to start two DPs in the 1960 Series.

1975—Answers

1. Bernie Carbo joined the Dodgers' Chuck Essegian (1959) as the only players ever to pinch-hit two home runs in World Series play.
2. Tony Perez hit two home runs in the fifth game, to lead the Reds to a 6–2 win.
3. Dwight Evans and Fred Lynn.
4. Denny Doyle became the fourth second baseman to commit three errors in a seven-game Series.

5. Tony Perez made the play, a feat last performed by Gordy Coleman in 1961.
6. Boston's Carlton Fisk made two errors in the third game.
7. Dave Concepcion and Cesar Geronimo.
8. Cincinnati's Rawly Eastwick joined Ross Grimsley as the only two relief pitchers of the 1970s to win two in relief in one Series, while losing none.
9. Luis Tiant (Boston) and Don Gullett (Cincinnati) each started three games in this Series.
10. Yaz went 9 for 27, hitting .310. Bernie Carbo hit .429 but he had only 7 at-bats.

1976—Answers

1. The Yankees' Otto Velez struck out three times in three at-bats.
2. George Foster did not steal a base but was caught twice.
3. Thurman Munson became the first player to accomplish this feat since Monte Irvin did it in 1951.
4. Davey Lopes led off the fourth and final game with a home run off Catfish Hunter.
5. Jim Mason played shortstop after Ellie Hendricks had pinch-hit for Chicken Stanley and Mason hit a home run in his first at-bat, his only trip to the plate in the Series.
6. Thurman Munson went 4 for 4 in a losing cause as the Yankees lost their fourth in a row to Cincinnati.
7. Cesar Geronimo and Joe Morgan stole two bases each.
8. Johnny Bench hit two into the left-field seats to help polish off the Yankees in the fourth game.
9. George Foster tied Eddie Roush's 1919 record. No left fielder ever had as many putouts.
10. The Yankees' Thurman Munson.

1977—Answers

1. Reggie Jackson had a slugging average of 1.250.
2. Reggie scored four runs.
3. Reggie Jackson.
4. Mickey Rivers went hitless in six at-bats in the opening game. He went 6 for 22 in the Series, hitting .222.

5. New York's Graig Nettles.
6. Mickey Rivers.
7. Thurman Munson and Reggie Jackson.
8. Mike Torrez tied the record last held by Larry Sherry.
9. Thurman Munson.
10. Duke Snider's record of fourteen extra bases on long hits was set in 1952.

1978—Answers

1. Reggie Jackson had a .767 slugging average in 24 games, consisting of two World Series with Oakland and two with the Yankees.
2. In the second game, Ron Cey hit a single, scoring Reggie Smith, and a three-run homer off Catfish Hunter in a winning 4–3 effort. Interestingly, Reggie Jackson had all three Yankee RBIs.
3. Davey Lopes's five RBIs on his two homers in the opening game helped L.A. to an 11–5 rout of the Yankees.
4. Reggie Jackson.
5. Don Sutton appeared in two games and gave up ten runs. He was the loser in both games.
6. Graig Nettles had three double plays in this Series, six in his career.
7. Catfish Hunter brought his total over six World Series to nine homers allowed.
8. It was neither Yeager nor Grote but Joe Ferguson in the ninth inning of game six.
9. Hooton, Sutton, and Hough.
10. Reggie Jackson was hit by Hooton and Forster.

1979—Answers

1. Kiko Garcia had a walk, two singles, a double, and a bases-loaded triple in the third game, to lead the Orioles to an 8–4 win. Only six players before Garcia had knocked in three runs with a triple, the last being Billy Martin in 1953.
2. The three Pirates were Dave Parker, Bill Madlock, and Willie Stargell. The Oriole was Kiko Garcia.
3. Willie Stargell. Pops also set a new record with seven extra-base hits, four doubles, and three home runs.

4. Doug DeCinces hit one into the left-field seats in the opening game, to help give the Orioles five runs in the first inning, all they needed in a 5–4 win.
5. Omar Moreno had 33 at-bats. He came through with 11 hits for a .333 average.
6. Phil Garner, the Pirates' second baseman, went 12 for 24, batting .500.
7. Doug DeCinces. The first was Fred Clarke in 1909, and the second was Babe Ruth in 1926.
8. Terry Crowley and Pat Kelly each went 1 for 4.
9. The Pirates' Tim Foli. He also was in on seven double plays in this Series, tying a record set by Pee Wee Reese in 1955 and 1956.
10. Pittsburgh's Phil Garner.
11. Pittsburgh's Kent Tekulve.